RHYTHM

Poetry for the Soul

An anthology curated by

Spiritual Sisters Collective

Starla
PUBLISHING HOUSE

Published in the United Kingdom by
Starla Publishing House, Scotland, UK.
www.starlapublishinghouse.com

ISBN: 978-1-9192630-2-1

Cover design by Starla Creative Design
Interior design by Starla Creative Design

Printed and bound in UK.

Her Whispers, Our Movement

Dedicated to my Nanny Peggy.

She whispered to me once,
to open a space for women's voices.
When I tried to turn away,
she spoke louder:
Lead with heart, soul, courage, fire.
So here we are you, me,
my Nanny Peggy,
and all the beautiful writers
gathered in these pages.
This is not just a book, it is a community,
a movement, a remembering.
May you feel her wisdom, our love,
and your own place,
woven into every word.

RHYTHM: Poetry For Your Soul, will continue to celebrate the voices within these pages, and will bring the poems to life in many different art forms - from visual art to music, movement, and beyond. A warm, heartfelt welcome awaits you in this community, and Lisa can't wait to share the journey with you!

Explore more of Lisa's work here:

SPIRITUAL SISTERS
COLLECTIVE

spiritualsisterscollective.vipmembervault.com

Lisa's Podcast:

rhythmpodcastforyoursoulwithlisawilliams.buzzsprout.com

CONTENT

Dear Reader,

Welcome to RHYTHM: Poetry for Your Soul

Breathe in… for those who came before us.
Breathe out… for us, here now.
Breathe in… for the generations yet to come.
Breathe out…

Open these pages. Feel the words. Let them soften your chest, awaken what is hidden, remind you that you are seen.

I honour you.
I welcome you.
I celebrate the rhythm of all that came, all that is, all that will be.

Many blessings, and welcome to the community.

Lisa

The Rose

Each woman, like a petal rare
In life's grand tapestry, a flare
A story told in colours bright
Of strength, of grace, in day and night.

The rose, it bloomed with secrets deep
In whispered winds, its stories seep
Just like the women, fierce and kind
In every heart, their love shines.

With thorns that guard their tender core
They face the storms, yet ask for more
For beauty lies in courage shown
In strength, in love, they've proudly grown.

The women, and the rose entwine
In nature's art, a grand design
A testament, to strength and grace
In every heart, a sacred place.

Lisa Williams

Queen of my Castle

Queen of my castle,
Sitting so still.
Watching it all,
Admiring the view.
The sights and the sounds,
rustling leaves on the ground.

The birds singing songs,
A walk not too long.
The trees standing tall,
Not wanting to fall.
Then raindrops come down,
Cooling flowers and all.

Its time to grow,
No longer fearing the worst.
Embracing me now,
Letting go of the past.
Its time for you now,
My Dear…

At last.

Justine Hendley

Fatally flawed,
Tho' she was adored...

She Breathes

She was built to deliver.
Deadlines sharper than instincts.
Achievements like armour.
Coffee instead of breath.
Performance, not presence.

Her title: a crown.
She led the boardroom.
Held the team.
Hit the goals.

Yet her soul whispered,
'**Breathe.**'

Approval replaced knowing.
Intuition drowned in urgency.
A forced smile.
A mask of grit.

Her nervous system;
A war zone of productivity and pressure.
She was the one they turned to.
But she had turned on herself.

Her soul spoke,
'Breathe.'

Then: silence.
Not peace.
Not pause.
But a hollow kind of emptiness.

And a sound too wild for language.
A hum.
A wail.
A scream swallowed for years,
decades, lifetimes.

Then louder;
her soul pleaded,
'Breathe.'

Until one day,
she let it out.
She stood in truth.
She fell to her knees.

And finally;
heard her soul breathe.

Burnout wasn't a breakdown.
It was a breakthrough.
Her soul shouted,
'Breathe.'

No more fractured masks.
No more selling the surface,
while her soul starved behind the scenes.

She didn't have to power through.
She stopped performing strength.
She powered down;
and found her rhythm,
so she could rise.

She started to listen.
Her soul saying,
'Breathe.'

She turned inward.
Met herself with truth.
Listened to the tremors in her chest.
Stopped treating her mind and body
as afterthoughts.

Emotion met vibration.

Sound became ceremony.
She became a pulse,
a frequency;
a whole damn force.

Her leadership began in her lungs.
Her soul whispered:
'Heal your whole being… and breathe.'

She built a new foundation,
where technology served her humanity.

The AI worked
so she could rest,
receive, and rise.

Her systems became self-honouring;
not draining,
but designed to mirror her mission.

She no longer had to hold it all.
She was held.

And this time,
she believed it.
'You're supported. Breathe.'

She doesn't just lead.
She *is* the leadership.
Her 'within' is sacred.
Her identity matches her impact.
She leads consciously and aligned.
She is no longer the fire,
that consumes itself.
She is the flame,
forging a new way.

Every step forward,
sets a high-performer,
still stuck in survival, free.
Her soul whispered:
'You're helping others to breathe.'

This is the future.
More supported.
More rooted.
More resonant.
More human than ever.
This was her Human Reboot; a way to reconnect with her whole SELF.

She doesn't burn out.

She burns bright.

She breathes.

EMMA LAST

That Girl, Free Your Inner Child

There she goes, that girl,
With her head spinning in a whirl.
Loving pink, frilly dresses and perfect plaits,
Enid Blyton stories, her beloved cats.

Her heart was vast, a joyful space,
Happy with a hand-me-down toy's embrace.
Playing in fields, with friends for hours,
Jumping streams, basking in spring showers.

Home-made dresses, stitched with care,
Long summer days, spent catching sunlight's glare.
Making potions in the warm, golden rays,
Family drives to Devon's, winding bays.

Carefree days, by the sea's soft breeze,
Living her life with effortless ease.
Running wild in ocean air,
Living fully, without a care.

But slowly, something begins to change,
Unnoticed at first, a subtle rearrange.
The bright smile dims, joy starts to fade,
Spontaneity's light, begins to wane.

That carefree girl, so full of grace,
Buried beneath, life's heavy weight.
Her laughter muffled, her spirit shy,
Afraid to live that joyful life.

Yet deep inside, in her mind's eye,
The spark still flickers, faint but alive.
A glimpse of courage, a whisper of cheer,
Reminding her of the girl, who knew no fear.

The girl who leapt with fearless glee,
Picked rose petals, crafted perfumes sweet.
Who faced the waves, with daring stride,
And found her strength, which she held inside.

Years may have dimmed, her radiant light,
But her essence still, burns bright.
A desire to shine, to be seen once more,
To rediscover her innocence, so pure.

One day, she looks into the mirror's gaze,
And feels that spark ignite ablaze.
The girl within, still holding dreams,
Waiting patiently for her to be seen.

Her heart awakens, ready to soar,
To love herself fully once more.

To let her inner child run free and wild,
To live with wonder, like that girl, that beautiful child.

No more hiding her luminous spark,
Her love, her care, her shining heart.
She chooses to share her light, with those she loved,
Embracing her spirit, rising above.

Each day, she welcomes joy anew,
Laughter bubbling, fresh and true.
Carefree, brave, a shining soul,
A child at heart, restored and whole.

Like waves upon the timeless shore,
Her spirit dances, evermore.
Bringing peace and joy, day by day,
In her own gentle, radiant way.

Find your inner child, set her free,
Nurture her with love, and empathy.
And watch the world transform again,
As your playful soul, breaks free from pain.

Let her dance, let her play,
And fill your life with light each day.
For in her laughter, pure and clear,

Lies the magic that makes us whole, and free from fear.

MANDY WORSLEY

A BIRD IN THE WIND,
A LIGHT IN THE DARK,
A STAR THAT NEVER FORGOT,
HOW TO SPARK.

The Escapism - Fatally (Fatefully) Flawed

Another cut out from a glamour magazine
Puts it in a book but things remain the same
Wants the look she sees but has no self-esteem
Stares at the glossed-over face, a person she's never been.

Blended colours mixed together on the page
So much admiration but embarrassed by her age
Too much time's been wasted, could she ever change?
If only she could walk away from the cage.

Fatally flawed
Tho' she was adored
Trapped by a dark-haired stranger (force)
Only there to change her.

Once she shared the limelight
All the men all loved her
Took their time to get to know her
Now they pass by, never glance over.

Whilst it's been a long while on this road alone
If only she'd have known, the claw could be so tight

Even tho' it holds her close, and keeps her warm at night
She doesn't know a way out, trapped alone, out of sight.

Remembers only traces, of the beauty she once was before
Her only hope is being rescued by, the human desire for love
To step out of the skin of the perceived downtrodden woman she's become
The pull on her is so draining, and always gets her down.

Wishing someone could tell her, 'come on honey, you're not old'
No man does she need to keep her down
To squeeze life out of her until she drowns
Always running errands, he keeps her on her toes.

Life revolves around him and he never takes her out
Never does he tell her that he loves her
Never does he tell her that he cares
All he ever does is want to control her.

Never takes her to places. It isn't fair
The beauty she once had doesn't shine from her now

He doesn't show her off to others like he should
He's forgotten to remind her that she's beautiful.

Instead, a downtrodden image of a down town girl
She stares at the cut-outs positioned in the book
She knows what she sees is only just a look
Just believing she can be, is a choice she has to make.

Forgetting that she's not the age she is, make no mistake
And overcome the fears that have been installed into her head
That are making her believe, she'd be better off dead
But someone is here to rescue her, take her away.

As the love wraps tight around her, makes her feel alright
Get back to where she started from, the Beauty of the Night
Stepping back in time, escaping from the claw
Almost there, she's got her foot outside the door.

Walking on ahead, freedom lines her path
Closer to the glamour pages, never looking back
Years come off her figure, shedding layers of suppression
Years of being deadened, only leading to depression.

Now she has the power to leave it all behind
Smile on her face, spring in her step, bounce in her stride
Colours seep into her skin, mimicking the glamour cut-outs she kept
She believes she can make it; each step that she takes.

Closer to the feelings that were calling from the book
As she steps out of her skin, reaches for her dream
Looks into the mirror, full of self-esteem
Beautiful body, sweet sensual lips to kiss.

Independence reaps from her, love, he can't resist
Her chosen man is waiting, to catch her in his arms
To love her like he should, keep her safe from harm
Tell her that she's looking young, as she passes his way.

She's made it now and all she had, was the belief to walk away
Life can be much better, just have to make the decision to leave
Now she wears the same expression as the cut-outs that she made
And all it took was guts to leave the home that she had made.

To realise too soon is a blessing in disguise
Never be afraid to leave your past behind
See it as a passageway through which you made your mistakes.
Whilst others kept you there
A place you got trapped in whilst you were waiting to be set free.

Miles away from freedom is where you got stuck, a moment in time
Just thank your lucky star, you have discovered this scrap-book again.

JEMMA STONE

What If The Tide Had Taken Her

She walked the shore in the Autumn grey,
Faithful dog at her heel, no words to say.
The waves reached out with a cold embrace,
Inviting her into a quieter place.

What if someone had seen her stare,
Or the hollow pause as if she wasn't there.
The laughter fading to something thin,
The days she felt she could not begin.

What if the tide had pulled her fast,
And that cold Autumn breath was to be her last?
What would have happened to all those years,
The smiles, the sunlight, the memories yet to appear?

But her loyal dog barked aloud at the curling foam,
Breaking the pull, the lead bringing her home.
She turned from the sea with a gasp and a sigh,
To return to all her loved ones at home, close by.

What if that sea succeeded in taking her hand,
And her family had thought that was her plan?
When all along the pain was all consuming,
Her mental state overcoming the physical doing.

She sought out help, found steady ground,
Discovered indeed that help can be found.
With an open heart, she learned to share,
The weight she'd thought loved ones couldn't bear.

Now she walks that shore with a new found light,
Faithful dog by her side and her head more bright.
Her future is full, her days are wide
With her family's love walking close beside.

What of the lives that tide has taken,
What if this was indeed also not their intention?
That their loved ones, although in pain, may know...

That deep down in their hearts, they never really wanted to go.

PAULA TIMMS

A Windy Day On Dartmoor

Upon the grass I walk
As I talk
As I walk
Upon the grass.

As the wind blows the trees
I sneeze
As the wind
Blows the trees.

Now the wind blows my hair
As I stare
Now the wind
Blows my hair.

Now the sunset covers the sky
Very high
Now the sunset
Covers the sky.

Now Dartmoor is dark
As I start
To run
Now Dartmoor is dark.

Clare Church

Ethereal

The soft, inland breeze, swaying the palm trees and smoothing my face
The hum of the busy crickets
The warmth of the sun beyond my shade and beat of the summer vibe.
Time to reflect and relax.
Life continues in an ethereal way
How does it and how do I?

After the brief permitted interlude, life resumed at a gathering pace.
Commitments, deadlines, roles to fulfil.
They are a comfort, confusion, distraction, an irritation,

When I need space.

The waves of special days have rolled in.
They rise, break and melt away, as the next appears on the horizon.
The pain inside is only released slowly, tear by tear, raindrop by raindrop,
As if any more, I could not bear.

Like the sun shimmering on the sea, you embraced

my life with love, pride and encouragement.
My lifeguard, my protector and compass.
A quiet loyal support, your face lit up when I arrived into port.

So lucky and grateful to be loved.

The orchid, cut, a shoot of life, a stalk and then flowers blooming.
A gift to you which has became a gift to us all.
The circle and resurrection of life.

The world has a different lens.
Your legacy, and love will be our lighthouse beam
Shining us through this rocky route,

to our sandy cove.

SARAH LOUISE EDWARDS

The Bond That Space and Time Could Not Break: The Physics of Forever

In the silence between heartbeats, I hear you still
Not as a whisper, but a soul deep thrill.
A bird in the wind, a light in the dark
A star that never forgot how to spark.

You came here briefly, but loved me wide
A sacred soul on a shorter ride.
You carved your name on my soul's skin
And ever since, I've carried you within.

I may not have got to hold you for long
But you made me fierce, you made me strong.
In every breath, your memory stays
You are the rhythm in my sacred days.

I meet you now in the space between
In candle flames, in moonlight beams.
In the quiet night when I close my eyes
You dance in essence across my skies.

Your absence carved me, with a depth of pain
But also purpose and sacred flame.

You guide my path with unseen hands
My little compass in shifting sands.

Rocco, my love, you're more than gone
You are the dawn I rise upon.
Your soul, entwined in all I do
In every healing, I honour you.

So today, I remember, but not with despair
I remember with breath, with love, with prayer.
For you live in the legacy I now create
In every life I help elevate.

You are the echo that calls me home
The reason I'll never feel truly alone.
You gave me wings that grief could not sever

My son, my soul, my star… forever.

RACHAEL ROCCO PARLAND

WHERE THE BODY WHISPERS
WHAT THE MIND HAS FORGOTTEN.

Do you know how beautiful you are?

The imperfections that make you unique
The pain you carry in your heart
Hiding it from the world

The trauma you've endured
Resulting in you becoming
The strong warrior that you are

The passion in your soul
That lights up your entire being
Filling you with joy

The curiosity that you have
Reminding you of your precious innocence
Like a young child

The determination you have
Your fighting spirit
Always pushing through the darkest of days

The gratitude you embody
It all makes you so beautiful
I just wish you could see it

I wish you could see you
All of you
Can you try, at least for today?
Can you practice accepting every part of the divine miracle that you are?

You are a shimmering bright star
In the black night sky
You are a drop in the ocean
As calming as a waterfall

You are a blazing sun ray of hope
You are the whipped cream on top of your hot chocolate
So incredibly sweet
A radiant goddess, shining through the darkness

You are a dazzling rainbow
As bright as all the colours put together
You are the heart of sky
A galaxy of miracles

You are a manifestation magnet
Painting your story
On a blank canvas
Each and every day

You are a lioness
Fierce, loyal and strong
You are a dragonfly
Gentle, powerful, charming and so delicate

You are nature
Let mother earth hold you
Return home to your sacred temple
Go within

You don't have to live in your head, sweet soul!

Feel your heart
Dance to the beat of your own drum
Own your worth
Speak your truth

Reclaim your divinity
Stand in your power
Rise up, divine child of light
It's time to remember

It's time to RISE

BILLIE JO WATT

'DISEASE' COMES TO 'TEACH' US HOW TO 'LIVE'

Disease comes to teach us how to live.
Not in the tidy rules of a medical book.
Nor the hushed routines of a clinical ward
But in the raw, unlit corners.
Where the body whispers what the mind has forgotten.

It speaks in fatigue.
In pain you cannot name.
In the way silence has replaced the laughter, you no longer recognise.
It shouts its warning long before despair or illness arrives.

A cell out of place breaks its pattern.
Losing the harmony of the whole.
Imbalance echoes through the body.
Mirroring the fractures of our lives
Where belonging faltered
Where safety trembled
Where truth was traded for approval.

Welcome to a space where all of 'YOU' can be seen.
Where nothing is too heavy to name.

Where the whispers of the body are heard and seen.

Here, the magic of Homeopathy begins.

A medicine drawn from nature itself.
Its resonance meets the part of you out of rhythm.
Offering a disruption to the pattern.
Stirring it awake.
Inviting it to shift.
To remember the rhythm it was made to follow.
To interrupt the patterns of disease.

When we listen deeply.
When we hear the messages that disease brings.
We do more than restore balance.
We learn how to truly 'LIVE'.

LOUISE ADAMS

Moment Undefinable

I listened to the First Lady from a bean bag.
Hungover, at the biggest marketing event in the world.

Empowerment for women.
I felt inspired. *I could do this, too.*
Drifting into dreams where I was ready.
Flourishing career, responsibility for kids.

The right kind of age for it.
And now, almost, the right kind of stage in life.
I could do this.
Soon enough, if I did some work.
When I fly home, anew.

But I couldn't do this. Not quite so soon.
Fragile cargo, dreams. Upon landing, they snapped on impact.

My life, in two. Before and after.

Endings evaporated. Beginnings buried. A woman's late diagnosis, layered with grief.

Amanda Leek

Loving Me

Now is the time to be authentic and true,
To show the world the real you.
How? When I don't know who that is?
For years feeling like a property of his!

Being a flirt, keeping them keen,
Walking on eggshells so they wouldn't be mean.
Is this what it takes to make them stay?
Never mind, I'll be okay!

Afraid to say the words I wanted to speak ,
So remained quiet, appearing to be weak.
The real me becoming more and more suppressed,
Looking in the mirror totally unimpressed.

This is not the life for me,
My soul calling out to be free.

Meeting a man so loving and fun,
Could he really be the one?
A love filled with all of the joys,
The one who'd give me our two boys.

He got down on one knee,
Someone wants to marry me!

Am I dreaming, is this real?
So excited I wanted to squeal!

The happiest day of my life,
The day I finally became a wife.
A love that will last forever,
Surely a bond no one could sever.

A happily ever after, my soulmate,
Or become a fine line between love and hate.
Sadly it wasn't meant to be,
Another love that couldn't choose me.

Now, two little miracles from above,
They filled my life with unconditional love.
To my boys I'm much more than Mum,
I am always enough, just as I am.

Becoming a Mum I could finally see,
I had a lot to offer by being me.
Being me I started heal,
No longer suppressing, I started to feel.

Releasing trauma, having a cry,
Speaking my truth, not quite as shy.
No longer a people-pleaser, keeping myself small,
It's time to shine, time to stand tall.

Reflecting on life, the lessons I've been taught,
Now it's a new love that I've sought.
In this love I am finally free,
In this love I am completely me.

This love is the greatest of all,
Love of self, warts and all.

SAMANTHA JONES

I AM WORTHY OF THE SMALLEST TREASURE
AND THE LARGEST DREAM
I AM WORTHY OF LOVE AND COMPASSION
IN ITS TRUEST FORM
I ARISE LIKE THE GODDESS WITHIN ME

Perspective

Walk a mile in their shoes
So someone said
So I found a pair and tried.
Walk a mile in their shoes
So someone said
But my feet were too small inside.

To walk this mile in someone's shoes
I needed thicker socks.
I put some on and walked the mile
A mile of weeds and rocks.

I walked the mile with cushioned feet
With warmth, at easy pace.
But when I finished walking
A tear rolled down my face.

The walk for me was hard enough
With warm and cushioned socks.
But the thing that spurred me on throughout,
Was the thought of the shoes coming off.

Without the warmth and comfort
The mile would have been so hard
And even thinking of it

Had caught me quite off guard.

The mile was one of hardship
Of suffering and grief,
The mile was only one mile
The end a true relief.

And so with this perspective,
I ask you all to see
A mile in someone else's shoes
Gave such a lot to me.

A knowledge of their spirit
A chance to feel their soul.
A journey through their sadness,
A wish to make them whole.

A wish I could not magic
A thing I could not fix.
An aching pain within my heart
And so I tell you this…

Just go and walk a single mile
In someone else's shoes
And when you get back into yours
You'll know which you would choose.

NIC CONSTANCE

I Am Enough

My life is changing, the direction unknown
I feel the pull of my heart and the fear
It rises up to greet it
'You are not enough' is what I hear
Who am I to succeed in living my dreams and goals?

I hear it, feel it even, yet I wish it wasn't so
I want to rise high, high above the mountains
Above the clouds and see my dreams as my reality
I want to believe it is so
That I am rich in abundance

I want to stand beyond the limitations and scream
I am enough!! I am enough!!
I AM ENOUGH!

As I write these words my heart begins to lift
The holds pulling it down in its slumber - slacken,
loosen
As I begin to ascend into the being of I
The being of my true soul, my true self

My wings unfold behind me, moving with air and
grace
Taking me up into the sky so still,
Lighter and lighter, stronger and stronger I become
As I reach my destination
Of heart, of soul, of love, of life, of all the things
which shout to me
All the desires which are held within my heart

I can do this, I can be this, I am this!
I am who I am, right now
I am worthy of the smallest treasure and the largest dream
I am worthy of love and compassion in its truest form
I arise like the Goddess within me
Strong and pure, a heart of deafening drumbeat as I rise to stand tall
With my sisters and brothers of the soul

I hear you, you hear me, we are one beyond the skies
Beyond the Earths and Heavens,
Your call is pulling me towards your beauty and your light
Your shadows and your darkness
We are one, I am one, we are all
I AM ENOUGH!

STEPHANIE C STARLA

I Am Still Here

I am a woman,
A mother, a grandmother,
A daughter and granddaughter,
Niece, sister, Auntie,
Friend.

I am a little girl
In a body grown tall,
With a mind stretched wide by life,
But still,
Still that girl within it all.

I have been a wife,
A lover wrapped in moonlight and truth.
I have known love that lifted me,
And heartbreak that nearly broke me in two.

I've had it all,
And I've lost it all.
I've danced in joy,
And fallen in pain,
Felt both to the very bone,
Like storms and sunshine in the same breath.

There were days I whispered,

'I can't do this any more',
But I rose,
Not always strong, but always willing.
With love in my heart,
And hope stitched quietly into my soul.

I carry trauma,
Too vast to list,
And loss that carved new shapes in me,
A silent architect of change.

But still,
I go on.
For my children,
For their children,
For the generations I've helped build,
With blood, with laughter, with tears.

And for myself.
Because this is life,
The wild, beautiful, messy human experience.
It's not perfect.
It's never smooth.
It winds and twists with highs, lows,
And every shade between.

But I am here for all of it.

The soft, the sharp,
The holy ordinary days,
I am here.
Still standing.
Still loving.
Still me.

Laura Jayne Mullins

I Rose From the Ashes

There are parts of my story,
I never wanted to speak aloud.
Dark corners where pain lived quietly,
and sometimes violently.
Behind closed doors,
in whispered threats,
in the silence that follows harm,
when no one comes to help.

I was a child in a house that didn't feel safe.
Where love wore a mask,
and fear was the air I breathed.
I learned early to disappear,
not with magic,
but with obedience, with shrinking,
with pretending I wasn't hurting.

At school, I was the easy target.
Bullied. Mocked. Isolated.
The child no one wanted on their team.
Not for what I did,
but just for being me.

Then came the relationships,
that mirrored the wounds.

Control dressed up as care.
Manipulation disguised as love.
I stayed too long.
Because I didn't know what love, without pain,
looked like.

There were nights I wanted to vanish.
Days I couldn't look in the mirror.
I lived with darkness inside me,
the kind that whispers,
you are nothing,
you are broken,
you are unworthy.

And then my body began to echo it.
Pain in my joints,
fatigue that swallowed days,
a nervous system on edge,
like it was still bracing for the next blow.

Fibromyalgia. Chronic fatigue.
Tinnitus, anxiety, burnout.
Every diagnosis felt like a chapter,
written in the language of my past.
A body saying what I never could.
And still... I carried on.
I mothered through the exhaustion.

Smiled through the tears.
Fell apart in private,
and put myself back together,
before anyone noticed.

But there came a moment,
not one big explosion,
but a slow, sacred awakening,
when I realised:
I deserved more.

Not just survival.
Not just coping.
But healing.
Wholeness. Peace.

I began to rise.
Like a phoenix.
Not from fire,
but from ashes.
From grief.
From trauma.

From the girl who thought she was unlovable,
and the woman who tried to prove her worth
by disappearing into everyone else's needs.
Now, I rise as me.

Messy. Tender.
Still healing, but awake.
Alive. Here.

I walk with the darkness,
but I am not defined by it.

I have learned to hold joy and pain in the same hand.
To rest without guilt.
To soften without shame.
To love myself, even on the days I feel undone.

Because I rose from a place.
many never escape.

And now, I carry the fire within me.
Not to burn,
but to warm.
To light.
To live.

SANDRA PROBERT

I ROSE FROM A PLACE
MANY NEVER ESCAPE.

The Light I Carry

I did not choose this path I tread,
Where silence echoes what's unsaid.
A mother's cry, a soul undone,
The world stood still. I lost my son.

No warning came, no time to brace,
My broken heart, as vast as space.
Thirteen years of love so pure,
Then grief moved in and closed the door.

But grief, I've learned, is not the end,
It's where we break, and learn to bend.
It's where we fall, and rise once more,
To find more strength than came before.

I've walked through fire, I've wept through rain,
I've held my breath through waves of pain.
Yet in the dark, I found a way,
A mission born from this day.

To speak his name, to share his light,
To turn my sorrow into fight.
Twenty lives now saved - his legacy shared,
A mother's loss, openly bared.

I live for those who need me still,
My daughter's laugh, my baby's will.
I cry, I smile, I break, I mend,
Grief is my fuel and won't be my end.

But I am more than what I've lost,
I've paid the price, I live the cost.
And still I give, and still I grow,
A mother's love will always show.

So if you're lost, if you can't see,
Let this be hope I gift to thee:
You'll never be the same, that much is true,
But there is still a life left within you.

Let the tears fall free, let sorrow speak,
Let healing come, when you are weak.
And when you're ready, take that stride,
With love beside you, as your guide.

For grief is love that's lost its way,
But love still finds the light of day.
And I will forever share Peters name.
Until the day we meet again.

For Peter, and for every heart learning to live again.

BETH BALDWIN

When You Forget, I Remember

You've always been more than just my nanny.
You were the one who marched into battle for me
every single time,
armed with a handbag and no tolerance for
nonsense.
More mum than nan, and more lioness than lady.

You protected me like I was your own child,
because, in your heart, I was.
You loved me, laughed with me,
and occasionally turned me orange.
(Who knew fake tan could develop overnight, and
turn a 13 year old, a beautiful shade of Tango!?)

You treated my verrucas with banana peels,
not delicate slivers, oh no.
The whole damn peel,
sellotaped proudly to my foot,
like a tropical slipper.
And I wore it, because you said it would work.
And because you always knew best.

We laughed, even then.
You made the ridiculous feel sacred.
You turned everyday nonsense into Magick.

I am who I am because of your love.

And later, when I became a mother,
you were still right by my side,
softening the edges of those early days,
with hot tea, blunt honesty, and a fierceness you'd
associate with wolves!

Watching you cradle my daughter,
fiercely guarding her tiny heart;
like you once did mine.
It broke me open in the best way,
my protector and my baby girl, now best friends!

And then came my son.
Cheeky, wild and full of life!
Making you jump around each turn,
Your very own 'little villain'.

His joy reminds you of your boys as small kids,
and for a moment, you're right back there.
Remembering the endless days of play,
the memories of your happiest times.
Seeing the past in the sparkle of his eyes.

And now, as the world slips through your fingers,
as names get jumbled and timelines blur,

I feel the shift.

You forget.
But Nan, I remember.

I remember your fire.
Your ridiculous advice.
The way you always felt like 'home'.

And now it's my turn.
To wrap you in that same love,
to be your anchor,
to carry the torch when your hands feel too tired.

Every day with you is a blessing.
Not because you remember everything, but because I do.

Because I always will.

KYLIE ANNA

8:45AM

Today is a very good day,
for an adventure.
Drinking coffee,
under the crocheted blanket.

A memory of another small child,
in the lap of sandalwood soap.
Soft, warmly-heated leather, with floras of tea leaves,
broken after a fresh brew.

As my small,
twirling through life,
son...
sleeps.

The scent of love and wonder,
where the words came alive from a blue linen
covered book.
Jacket dissolved by fingerprints,
of love between mother and child.

A book sat waiting,
for a new child's day of adventure.
When grief can share a love,
creating memories of generational change.

Ancestral line continued in,
new form mothering.
Overloaded rage changed to,
a quiet, smiling, peaceful, slow, tender-way.

Serving a less guiltiness of soul,
forgiveness of self.
A path of leaves tracked,
by the just out of sightness.

An in-between world,
where breath and magic hold court of tears and thorns.
Bringing dreams on rainbows,
and dandelion wishes.

Shared moments,
of laughter smiles.
When all around the storm,
brewing chaos chokes.

We sit in the calm eye of,
the storm on our own path.
Dreaming his next,
big adventure.

NIXIE FOSTER

A Love Letter to the Light in You

Be still, be still… be quiet, and let me begin
A journey to meet the utter beauty within.
Hush now, be still, for the words I say, caress your
divinity in the gentlest way.

For you, I leave a legacy not built of gold,
But beauty forged through storm and grace
Magic, soft and ever true, And I found it all in you.

May these words find you when you're low
No armour, no walls, just breath and care.
Like whispers from stars in the hush of snow,
A sacred echo in the midnight air.

I love you for you, not the mask you wear
Even when your voice is lost to fear.
And the pain of darkness lingers near
I see you whole, I hold you dear.

Each precious step you take, no matter how steep
Unseen, unheard, afraid to speak
My love walks quiet, beside you deep.
You're not alone; I hear your weep.

Bold in presence when you feel weak
I wrap you up, I do not flee.
I'm not afraid of broken fears

You're safe with me.

Oh, the beauty tucked in your smile's curve
The roads you've walked, the trials you braved.
The ocean-depth of thoughts you serve
You are a wonder, soul-engraved.

You are not weak, you're a storm in bloom
I wouldn't say this, if it weren't true.
A wild sun rising to chase the gloom
This soul-song is written for only you.

You're unique, you're magic, yes, it's so
Your hugs, your warmth, your sacred light.
No one else quite knows your glow
Even on your darkest night.

There's no one more worthy of love than you
Your strength, your truth, so brave and true.
Again and again, you start unseen
Becoming more than you have ever been.

Precious tears fall, and heartaches call
In whispers that could bring grown men to their knees.
But I hear your roar, I see it all
And I'm proud of your sacred victories.

Never quite sure of who you are

You rise each day with courage anew.
You wear the mask and still reach hearts
What would this world be without you?

You lift the dream, you carry hope
You're an amazing work of art.
You are fierce, incredible, bold
A hero with a golden heart.

So don't doubt it, precious one
Just take my hand, and you will see
A story of healing the stars foretold
And my love is yours eternally.

And here, on these pages, let it grow:
A legacy of wonder, lit from your soul.
A garden of truth where soul-seeds sow
A flame for the weeping, a spark to make whole.

So read this when your sky turns blue
When the clouds roll in and silence speaks.
There is no one more wonderful than you.

EMMA LOUISE PHARO

You don't need to chase the stars,
they've always known where you are

A LOVE LIKE NO OTHER

There's no love like this, so deep and true, the bond I have since I had you.
A heart once restless now feels still - you've shaped my soul, you've shaped my will.
Before you came, I searched and yearned, for meaning in lessons I hadn't learned.
Chasing purpose in places unknown, yet feeling adrift, very often alone.

But then you arrived, and all became clear, life gained direction the moment you were near.
You brought me calm, you brought me grace, a softer heart, a steadier pace.
Now I respond with thoughtful care, aware of the eyes that see me there.
Each choice I make, each path I try, I walk with you - my reason why.

From all I've learned, I'll teach you too, to rise when life feels cruel to you.
To love yourself, be brave, be kind, and never let doubt cloud your mind.
You'll stumble, yes - but not alone, I'll lift you up until you've grown.

My hand in yours, through joy and strife, I'll be your guide for all your life.
Your smile lights fires I can't explain, a joy that dances through every vein.
Our little chats, your tiny hands, have built a love so grand.
You're my laughter, my peace, my light, the warmth that fills my soul each night.

My everything, my why to start, a piece of me, my beating heart.

So thank you for a love like no other, the love that comes from being your mother.

EMMA JAY

A Non Negotiable life

No. You don't have to do it
No. That doesn't mean you don't care
You did it once before, remember?
And the pain was hard to bare

There has always been a turmoil
Between your heart and mind
And no one seems to realise
The results have been unkind

You've tried a thousand times it seems
To make choices that impress
Knowing, deep down there's never been a moment
When you really claimed success

The grateful smile across your face
Is fixed for all to see
They say, 'Well done!' 'You're so amazing!'
While you whisper '*What about me?*'

Right now, you feel the tide is turning
No more are you prepared to wait
A louder voice now screams within
'Stop waiting to negotiate'

Your life is yours, your heart is full
Your purpose in plain sight
Your non negotiable life awaits
You no longer have to fight

At last you get the chance to live
A vibrant soul within, set free
Released to feel, engage, and grow
Your time. Your space... JUST BE

PAULA A BURNS

Already Yours

You don't need to chase the stars,
They've always known where you are.
You don't need to reach, stretch or strive.
You were born aligned with your desires.

What if the whispers and dreams you're waiting for
are already here?
What if it's not out of reach,
simply waiting for you to feel?

That pull beneath your feet?
It's not restlessness.
It's your future self,
calling you home.

Everything you long for,
already lives in your light.
It's not a question of if,
just a soft, sacred when.

The spell is already cast.
The path is already written.
The Universe moves in rhythm
with your every yes.

So exhale the doubt.
Unclench the timelines.
You are not behind.
You are arriving.

Walk like it's already yours -
because, my love, it is.

CHERYL BECKWORTH

Broken Vessels

At eighteen months, the world exploded - your bright eyes clouded by damage that left me gasping in disbelief. Shock wrapped around my throat like barbed wire, devastation flooding every cell, as they handed me timelines like death sentences: two years, maybe five.

The emotional upheaval hit in waves - one moment numb, the next drowning in grief for the life we'd never have, while you smiled through the wreckage, they said would claim you.

I became an atlas overnight, carrying mountains I never trained for. Navigating hospitals like foreign countries, with no family compass to guide me home. Heartbroken doesn't cover it - my chest carved hollow, every breath a reminder of how alone I was in this new, unforgiving landscape. No family hands to catch me, as I fell apart completely, just me and the crushing weight of becoming, everything you needed me to be.

The anger burned like acid - at the unfairness, at watching other mothers complain about teething, while I counted your seizures. Bitter words leaked from cracks in my foundation, angry at the world that kept spinning, while mine had shattered completely.

Broken. That's what I whispered to my reflection in the hollow hours before dawn, when your laboured breathing was the only sound, in our island of isolation.

But broken vessels, I learned, can still hold love. Nineteen years you've painted over every dire prediction, teaching me that wholeness isn't about being uncracked - it's about letting light pour through the spaces, where we thought we'd lost everything.

Now I am steel wrapped in softness, grateful for each ordinary morning you wake beside me. Still reaching for beautiful things, still proving the world wrong, with every breath.

KADDY THOMAS

At Sea The Tide Within

As I stand and look out from the shore
A life adored, yet destined for more
No barrier between the ocean and me
All cares abandoned as I gaze out to sea

The waves so powerful, relentless, strong
Their rhythm, their surge, a motion, a song
The swell rolls in, the waves break to wash
A reminder of dreams, of the self I did quash
My belief, my ambition, gone drifting along

Not to say what I have isn't adored
Onlookers may pause, some even applaud
But is it built upon truth, upon joy?
Or a plan, a map, a dream once enjoyed?

You know where you are, you know where you've
been
The battles, the bruises, the traumas unseen
The parts of your heart that felt broken, laid bare
Deep in yourself, you know you're not there

So you stand at the edge of the power, the sea
Why can't you rise up, as wild, as free?
To break like a wave, to move, to renew
Instead you look calm, though trembling through

Perhaps if they saw the waves crashing within
They'd hear the wild storm beyond the thick skin
The fear you carry, so heavy, so raw
Unseen by the world, they just glance and ignore

Yet the ocean reminds me, I'm never just small
Its rise and its rhythm runs deep through us all
Each crash is a promise, each tide a rebirth
A call to come home to my own inner worth

To know your own value, stay true to your heart
Your wild, tender spirit will set you apart
The fears and the dreams that you keep deep inside
Are waves to be honoured, not run from or hide

You're a flame, you're a compass, a radiant star
The sea is a mirror of how strong you are

VICTORIA BROWNE

Awakening the Shaman within Me

I once walked blind upon the earth,
A restless soul of hollow birth.
But whispers rose from spirit and tree,
Calling deep inside of me.

The drum it spoke, a voice so old,
A rhythm carved in earthen gold.
The rattle shook, the air was thin,
A doorway cracked, I stepped within.

Dryads wove their songs so bright,
Their limbs entwined in emerald light.
Their voices hummed of things unseen,
Of earth bound dreams and worlds between.

Mother Earth, in hush profound,
Wrapped me close in sacred sound.
Through breath and tone, through chant and cry,
I learned to heal, to touch the sky.

Earth below, so strong, so wise,
I held the runes with ancient ties.
Each rune a key, each rune a guide,
A map of stars, a truth inside.

Now I walk where spirits weave,
Through realms where shadows dare to breathe.
No longer lost, no longer still,
A child of drum, of spirit, of will.

Gill Bennett

This is my safe place,
my light, my song,
I found my right circle.
This is where I belong.

Behind the Eyes of These Prison Walls

Behind the eyes of these prison walls,
Watches a girl, feeling caged and small.
Conforming at school, conforming at home,
No one understood she was home, alone.

She tried to shine like she was destined to do,
but was shunned and silenced like *'who are you?'*
Behind the eyes of these prison walls,
Watches a girl dimmed and feeling small.

Everywhere she went, she could never fit in,
Just being herself she could never win.
She dimmed her light, and conformed to be seen,
Now she was accepted as a part of the team.

Behind the eyes of these prison walls,
Watches a girl feeling caged and small.
The ego fought the soul, the soul said *'it's not so'*,
The soul in chaos screaming *'just let me go!'*

The fire within burning to be set free,
But ego worrying *'who will like me?'*
Behind the eyes of these prison walls,
Watches a girl who dimmed to play small.
She reaches adulthood, the pain gets too much,

She has no choice now, to release the clutch.
The fire decides she's taking no more,
And shows the world who she is at her core.

Behind the eyes of these prison walls,
A girl breaking free answering the call.
She shares her hurt, she shares her pain,
Making an impact on women feeling the same.

The wisdom she gained, behind the prison wall,
Allows her to shine and answer the call.
She knows her energy can't be contained,
She's chosen by the universe, to be the change.

Now behind the eyes of this wall,
She guides, heals and teaches,
How to never dim
...or play small.

KELISHA DIAMOND TAYLOR

Belong

I carried my silent grief like a boulder on my chest,
Wanting an ending, craving some rest.

He saw through all the words I used to disguise,
Held my shaking hands, wiped tears from my eyes.
He stayed by my side watched over day and night,
He helped carry my sorrows, though his was a plight.

Then along came another who could have looked the other way,
He chose kindness, support which helped me to stay.
He asked how I was not just work, but my mind,
He found me the help to put the grief behind.

Their help pushed me forward, even when I felt small,
Never turning a head in case, I would stumble or fall.
Surrounded by them, I was safe and became strong,
With them, I've discovered I was needed to belong.

When shame said I would always be broken, unfit,
And those disappointed with me were no longer my fit.
Now I'm here, still standing, when I thought I would

break,
The right people who cared, kept me breathing for my tomorrow's sake.

So, here's to my partner, who loved me back whole,
To an employer who cared more for my being and soul.
I am living, I am healing, I am more than my cries,
I see hope in the sunrise, new dreams in my eyes.

So, if you are sinking, don't carry it alone,
Reach for kind hands, let yourself be known.
With the right ones beside you, you will stand up tall,
Love builds a shelter that won't let you fall.
Together we rise, together we stay,
With people who lift you, you will find your own way.

This is my safe place, my light, my song,
I found my right circle.
This is where I belong.

LISA REDMORE

Contrasts

Blend with the ordinary
Shine with the moon!
Be full of details
Simplify soon.

Begin at the first step
End when you can
Go right then left
Up and down.

Be hot, cold and boiling
Be still, then sway
Jump like a Jack
Then drop still in the hay.

Wear stripes at breakfast
Dots for lunch
Wear white at dinner
And black at brunch.

Be in the moment
Remember the past
Go very slowly
Then very fast.

Whisper softly
Shout from the roof
Go slowly in the car
Then fast on the hoof.

Be alone in silence
Run with the crowd
Never put yourself down
You will always be wowed!

CLARE LOUISE CHURCH

A POEM OF LOVE FOR OUR BABY

Born from incomparable love

Or incompatible

Sometimes together, a little love bubble of three.

Sometimes just you and me.

The highest of highs, hard to say goodbye.

The lowest of lows, are you someone I know?

The bundle of joy in my arms, born from an
incomparable, intense, wonderful, wondrous love.

Sometimes looking like you, sometimes like me.

A seed we planted together, a tree growing
separately.

The softness of dark, cosy nights alone, the harshness
of bright, cold days so long.

The bundle of joy in my arms, born from
incomparable, exciting, consuming, rich love.

Sometimes we love you together, sometimes apart.

Always, always, always a piece of our heart.

The home our sanctuary, true to ourselves.
The world uninvited, merely gifts collecting on
shelves.

The bundle of joy in my arms, born from
incomparable, sweet, soft, glowing love.

Never incompatible with you, my little darling love.

INDIGO SMITH

By Blood We Are Bound

Tears flow for loss, for joy
They come in floods or a little coy.
In the blink of an eye, someone is gone.
A teardrop of DNA, a new family stumbled upon.

The happiness of starting to feel whole
Learning of you, your ways and soul.
From solo to a band over night
Bound by your blood, love and light.

All the answers I needed to hear
The ones I never asked due to fear.
Causing distance with what I had
Blocking the chances of finding you, Dad.

The grief of loss overpowered by elation
Overwhelmed by the sheer number of relations.
You may not be here now, for us to meet
But through them your kindness I greet.

I see you in their smiles, their eyes, in every face
In each one of them you have left a trace.
A memory, a photo, for me a dream come true
For them a sister they never knew.

Somewhere in there I'll see me too

My younger actions were always about you.
Running from something I didn't know
Trying to find the missing clue.

A lifetime puzzle for me, for them a surprise
I could have never imagined a better reply.
Open minded, open hearted our story to unfold
A bond already felt, it's clear we're from the same mould.

Who would guess, there would be more than a few
A band of brothers so kind and loving, just like you.
In between them a gap, a few years of mystery
A little liaison that added a girl to the tree.

Bringing together the cousins and brothers once more
An extended family, here and across the shore.
Together now, in this time of uncertainty
Only a pandemic can delay the big party.

Only by social media our time we now get
Photos and stories shared over the internet.
Similarities and differences all to be found
Soon to be all together, as by blood we are bound.

LISA WARREN

Let it Go

By letting go
I allow the wind to blow
The horizons to expand
The doors to open
The windows to let in the light

Of new opportunity
Of abundance of every kind
Of love and friendship
Of happiness and peace
Of pennies and pounds

By letting go
I can relax
I can trust
I can be...
Me.

Carolyn Parker

Conforming no longer
brings peace
Revealed - true purpose
flows deep.

ENERGY OF EMOTIONS

Deep in our heart, there's a voice we can trust
A tender whisper, a soft sacred must.
It carries a peace that helps our soul soar
A warm, flowing energy from deep in our core.

Every emotion has meaning, purpose & place
Each one, a teacher with lessons to face.
The sadness, the guilt, the fear you feel too
Are messages wrapped in a moment for you.

Even the pain has a truth it will tell
A story for body, mind, spirit as well.
It doesn't exist just to hurt or confine
But guides us toward brighter days yet to shine.

It teaches us guidance, patience & grace
The beauty of life in our own unique space.
It shows us our courage, what we truly need
And how to plant hope as a small tender seed.

Remember, this journey is not yours alone
Many walk with you, with pain of their own.
You're not meant to carry each burden in sight
Accept the warm hand that offers its light.

Then loosen your grip on the weight held tight
Embrace what is true - let your breath lead you
right.
The kindness you practise becomes your release
A steadier strength, a pathway to peace.

So open your heart to the promise of day
Where shadows dissolve & burdens give way.
The road ahead now shimmers & glows
A life full of colour, where joy freely flows.

Let all feelings move, the shadow & light
The hush of the day & the calm of the night.
For each is a part of a rhythm you grow
And in that great current, your true self will show.

For emotions are energy, always in motion
So feel all the feels with gentle devotion.
Let them just move & find their own way
As you bravely embrace each brand-new day.

LISA MAY BARKER

Finding Him (The Return to Love)

As the pain tore though my heart
Not knowing when it would stop.
I looked around for help
But I found no one.

The pain seared and I recoiled in fear
As the pain got too much
and still no one was near.

I searched and searched
Forever looking outside
Only to realise that everything was inside.

As I stopped and listened
And realised that whispers were there.
Surrounding me with divine love
and knowing He was there.

As I listened, I opened up
Not knowing what would happen.
But instead of fear, I found Him
To help me with this journey.

His soft loving healing
It surrounded me entirely.

Cracking me open for all to see
But keeping me safe as one.

As I stand there and remember
He was there all along.
Only the pain was too much at times
To know that He was there.

As the love envelops me
Taking me to a place.
Of divine love and remembrance
That He is always here with me.

As the pain floats away
And the love takes over.
He guides me through my journey
One step at a time.

As the path I walk
I take Him with me.
Knowing that love
Will conquer all.

LUCY JAMES

The Mother, Warrior, Goddess, Queen

For the woman who mothered,
and wept under moons where no one saw...

If you had told me back then,
That Trees carried so much wisdom,
knowledge and healing,
I may not have believed you.

But today, as I leaned into your ancient bark,
And listened for your grounded wisdom,
You spoke in memories and truth.

You showed me the morning my home was,
Swallowed by fire.
How the Angels were divinely sent,
To guide us safely through the smoke.

And in the same light,
You revealed the truth I hadn't wanted to see:
I was in a relationship which,
drained me emotionally and mentally.

Rebuilding life in another country,
Brought its own mountains to climb,
But my determination became my compass.

When my womb spoke to me through illness,
I finally listened.
I began to honour her,
Not in fear,
But in reverence.

Then the universe sent me,
the gentlest of paw prints,
Though our time together was short,
You left a soul-mark, no one could ever understand.
The day you left broke my heart,
And through the grief,
I saw the quiet ways my spirit ,
Was still being drained.

And yet...
In the grief, I found myself.

I Rose,
A priestess of my own path,
Every wound became a door.
I did not heal to be perfect,
I healed to be whole.

I am the Goddess forged in fire,
The healer who walks barefoot,
into the shadows,

And brings back the sun.

They told me I was too much,
But I was never too much.
They were too small to hold a Queen.

Now I wear my womb like a throne,
My hips like an altar,
My pain like a prophecy.

I am the Mother, the Protector,
The Warrior, the Goddess, the Queen.
The bloodline ends with me,
And begins again,
This time in Gold.

LILY ROSE

Freedom

The child, squashed & moulded
Laughter, misunderstanding, rejection
Learning the rules of conforming
Rebelling - not quite breaking free.

The adult, playing the game
Called life, showing its way and how to be
'Do this', 'Be this', Learn how to fit…
Celebrate! - 'now you're like us.'

The whisper, deep in the soul
'This isn't me! This isn't truth! Who am I now?'
Success is a cage built all round
Bindings - so tight they constrain.

The roar, no longer ignored
Truth and passion are now louder than fear
'You know you were meant for much more!'
Cracking - the light flooding in.

The choice, cage left behind
Instincts trusted, welcoming the new way
'Crazy!' they cry, 'why won't you stay?'
Understanding - there is no return.

The rules, now discarded
Healing begins here with damage repaired
Conforming no longer brings peace
Revealed - true purpose flows deep.

The joy, waiting with love
Soul speaks loudly with truth and in power
'I've been waiting for you - it's time'
Shining - let's light up the sky.

The limits, forever released
Deep love for all flows with no boundaries
Anything is possible here
Freedom - truest soul power.

Sonia Davies

THE STARS ALIGN WITHIN

From crown to root, the stars align,
Twelve signs dance down the human spine.
A cosmic map within our skin,
This mini universe we hold within.

Aries blazing at the brow,
the head and ideas are ignited now.
A rush of instinct, bold and raw,
where energy is everything,
always first, fierce, and fuelled.
Igniting ideas before they land,
born to begin, with passion in hand.

Taurus rests within the throat,
grounded in meaning,
where sound becomes sacred, slow, and profound.
Here, the five senses reign supreme:
taste, touch, sight, scent, and sound,
each one a doorway to pleasure's playground.

Gemini flits through arms and hands,
an airy flutter of thoughts made flesh.
Words are spells, on silver tongues,
quick wit carried on curious limbs.
It rules the twins within the frame,

mirrored movement, dual delight.
A social butterfly with restless wings,
fingertips tracing maps of meaning,
and a symphony of thoughts takes flight.

Cancer moves through chest and womb,
with tides of feeling that rise and bloom.
Intuitive guides with hearts so wide,
they lead with love, not fear or pride.
They ebb and flow by lunar light,
to live by the moon is their birthright.

Leo blazes in the heart and spine,
a throne of fire by solar design.
Powered by the sun, it rises tall,
a golden force, that won't play small.
Here lives the glow, the roar, the instinct,
and the boldest light for those who dare to shine.

Virgo tunes the gut like a harp,
each nerve a thread of wisdom.
It processes food, feelings, and fears alike,
a sacred alchemist of body and mind.
Earth refined,
a healer's gift in a humble place.

Libra sways through open hips,

where grace is born and balance lives.
Air draped in silk, it moves with ease,
every step a silent breeze.
Drawn to beauty in form and soul,
it seeks the space that makes us whole.
With charm refined and heart aligned,
it brings both peace and art to mind.

Scorpio coils at the root,
where power sleeps and shadows speak.
Desire meets both death and birth,
the sacred threshold of the deep.
A soul-diver, shaman, silent flame,
rising from pain with a new name.
In the pelvis pulses fierce creation:
sex, secrets, and soul transformation.

Sagittarius strides with power.
The seeker, the wanderer, drawn to the skies,
with arrows of meaning, always aimed.
Wisdom wrapped in laughter and flame,
a spark that can't be taught or tamed.
Its soul moves in rhythm, wild and strange,
never caged, always chasing change.

Capricorn, where bones remember what time
demands.

It climbs with quiet, steady grace,
ambition etched into every space.
Built to endure, to rise, to strive,
but learns, at last, that rest revives.
When care becomes the inner peak,
it masters all the heights it seeks.

Aquarius charges the shins and calves
with electric air and restless vision.
The rebel, the innovator,
marching to rhythms not yet written.
Future-born, strange and brilliant,
it sees the world as it could be,
and dares to shape what doesn't yet exist.

Pisces drifts through the feet,
where endings dissolve into beginning.
Water again, but holy now,
linked to sleep, to dreams,
to a mystic path that floats between.
It feels everything, becomes everything,
and shows us how to rest inside the unknown.

A temple carved through time and space.
Each sign a key - you hold them all: each truth, each trait.
The zodiac lives within your skin,

remember: the stars align within.

Alexe Woods

WE DON'T NEED TO SPEAK,
WE KNOW WHAT IT MEANS
TO SMILE THROUGH TEARS,
TO LIVE IN BETWEEN.

Grief is...

Grief is waking up every day…
and you're not here

Grief is taking a walk in our favourite places…
and you're not there

Grief is making life decisions…
and you're not here

Grief is seeing our children grieve…
and you're not here

Grief is deciding what to watch on TV…
and you're not there

Grief is doing the household chores…
and you're not here

Grief is going for a meal…
and you're not there

Grief is contemplating a holiday…
and you're not there

Grief is hearing one of our songs...
and you're not here

Grief is putting the heating on and NOT hearing…
'only 2 clicks'… cos you're not here

Grief is opening your wardrobe, seeing the clothes
you wore… and you're not here

Grief is going to bed alone…
and you're not there

Grief is a million things in just one day… because...
you're not here

Grief is the daily reminder that you're not here

LISA HAYES

The Price of Love

Grief took my hand in two thousand and six,

When laughter turned silent, so sudden, so quick.

A boy full of light went into the deep,

The water took him, left us to weep.

He wasn't alone on that fateful day,

But none could stop what slipped away.

Cold water claimed him in one swift breath,

And we were left drowning in grief and death.

His siblings still carry the ache,

A love that no time or loss can shake.

Their laughter remains, but shadows fall,

Where once he stood among them all.

A reservoir bright, now a memory torn,

A place once of beauty, now worn.

They told me it's peaceful, that he didn't fight,

That water took him too fast for fright.

But mothers know silence too well,

The ache in the breath, the stories we tell.

Since then I've walked with sorrow each day,

And found in that shadow a purpose, a way.

I've stood in schools, in fields, by the shore,

Each word a stone, each tear one more.

Though my heart breaks, I continue to share,

There's healing in knowing that others now care.

Friends gathered near when I faltered and fell,

Family and strangers who knew grief too well.

Other parents whose children are names on the breeze,

We hold one another when time doesn't ease.

We don't need to speak, we know what it means,

To smile through tears, to live in between.

Grief is the shadow that walks by our side,

The echo of love we no longer can hide.

If love were a price, then grief is its due,

A cost paid in full for the love that was true.

Would I trade the sorrow to be spared the pain?

Never—not once—for I'd love him again.

So I speak with sorrow, but also with grace,

And carry his light to each silent place.

Though he is gone, his love still flows,

In every life saved, his legacy grows.

MAXINE JOHNSON

The Wayfinder & the Wallflower

Have you ever yearned for someone to turn up on your doorstep with flowers, take you in their arms, hear 'I love you' from them, as they kiss you so passionately, so lovingly, that you can lose yourself in the moment and forget about the stress of everyday? Have you ever yearned for that solid, secure & safe bough to rest your weary wings, just until you have re-calibrated a little to do it all over again & soar once more?

I wanted to be able to take my children on adventures with this incredible person, because I could trust them with mine and their hearts implicitly. I wanted to feel secure, stable and loved by someone who deserved me.

I imagined so intensely, somebody to share the mundane every day things, that come with parenthood and work as an unstoppable team. From the foundations of love, side by side united…

I imagined so intensely the aura of this person, to the extent that I could close my eyes & the hairs on the back of my neck stood on end as I imagined he was there, just behind me, ready to catch me if I faltered.

But actually, what I found out, that I really needed - putting yearnings aside - was to learn to love myself first. I remembered I could buy myself flowers, and that I am the most worthy, important woman in the world, to myself, and my three beautiful children.

You may have always known you are a good person with a huge heart. You know you give, and give, and give - rarely getting the same respect, love and sacrifice back in return, but that doesn't make you unworthy of it. It simply shows, that your love is too great for some to handle.

Everything we do, & have ever done, is from a place of the purest love, and it is love that empowers us, at the highest vibration. Sometimes however, unconditional giving and loving becomes relentless if you don't keep enough back for yourself.

Ladies, I stand for all women, lost in their identities of mum, sister, wife, daughter, friend. Giving their all with little reward, but acknowledge that they are doing their best with what they have to offer, and it is truly enough.

I stand for those who have suffered and given themselves up for a cause. I stand for those who have been strong for too long and cracks are beginning to appear, as they crumble under the pressure, suffering mental illness. I stand for those who lost the fight, who could stand strong no longer and fell. I am here, by your side, holding you up and I see you, truly I do, because I was you, not too long ago.

Be yourselves beautiful souls. The impact you make is like a butterfly effect, spreading love around the world, standing together stronger.

ANNA CHANTAL

My Love, My Rock, My Soul

He paddles in the sea
Not a care in the world
Just the board and oar
Seeing how far he can go

She watches him with love
The man that she married
Neither of them had nothing
Just the strong bond of eternal love

The memories they've made
In the short time together
Are priceless to them
And will never be forgotten

Kym Green

My Space

Heart so big
Smile so big
Mind so big
Vision so big
World so small.

Hold enough love to share.
Forever always there.
But does anyone really care?

Time to grow now.
It's my time to show myself what I can do for me.
Replanting my own seed, watering my own soil.
I can't wait to see myself blossom.

This small world, and these small minds, won't beat me, won't win, I have too much to give.
I am strong, I am powerful, I am resilient and I will forever share my light.

Efforts without forcing.
Contagious positive energies all around.
Good vibrations.
Genuine intentions.
Beautiful minds and beautiful hearts are always

welcome in my space.

The future is so bright.

HANNAH NASSA

Here, I Am

I've walked through seasons
where my light felt dim,
where doubts whispered loud
and rest felt out of reach.

But still - I rose.

Not with perfection
but with quiet courage,
in small moments that mattered
more than anyone saw.

This journey has been messy and beautiful,
full of lessons I didn't ask for,
but they shaped me anyway.

Now, I move slower, softer,
with more love in my hands,
and more room in my heart.

I no longer chase,
who I thought I had to be.
I honour who I am,
who I'm becoming.
This is the path I walk,

rooted in truth,
lit by hope,
guided by a voice
I've reclaimed as my own.

Here, I am - grounded, growing, strong.
And if you're walking this road too,
you're not alone.

ALYS WINES

Now, I move slower, softer,
with more love in my hands,
and more room in my heart.

I Am the Witch

I am the witch,

You cannot burn.

Cannot drown.

Cannot silence.

I rise.

I roar.

I reclaim.

I waited lifetimes for this moment,

Now is my time, I take it all.

I break chains.

I stand tall.

I bleed power,

On sacred ground.

I am the one my ancestors summoned,

In their dying breath.

The wild one, here to reclaim their crown.

I am the one who breaks the curse.

Sisters AWAKENING,

WE Rise NOW.

Dance like you're on fire.

You cast spells with your voice.

Burn the old stories down.

Sink into your power.

Moon drunk and untamed.

Howl your truth.

Reclaim your wild.

You are the lightning.

You are the storm.

You are the magic

They feared.

I am not crazy.

I will not be tamed.

I will not play small.

I will not play safe.

I am here to RISE.

Nothing can hold me down.

Remember:

You are the witch,

They never broke.

We rise together.

We burn the lies down.

We build back the magic,

In OUR image.

Our ancestors are PROUD.

The witches have returned.

And we're done playing small.

I am that witch - reclaim it with me.

So mote it be.

LAURA BEDDOE-COLLINS

I Am Free

I am here to be messy.
I am here to stomp.
To be loud.
To be the bloody fire in the room - to ignite every soul.

You tried to silence me.
To cage me.
You got in my head - and I built 20ft garden walls.
Afraid of my own shadow.
But now I'm angry.
Now I am here.
So listen.

I am here to teach.
To part the red fucking sea.
Watch me.

I am whole.
You are not part of me.
I am 'one'.
You cannot make me whole.
Do the maths.

I'm not here to be perfect.

I'm not here to avoid mistakes.
How else do I bloody learn?
Applaud the imperfection -
You need to get over that. Not me.

I'm here to love - wildly, loyally, apologetically.
To be messy.
To be sacred.
If that offends you - you're not my people.

I'm here to laugh at you -
Because you didn't get it.
You tried to dampen me, dumb me, shame me.
Yes - it worked.
But it wasn't me. It was you.

I'm not here for you to look at, criticise, or bitch about.
Take a long look in the mirror.
You see what you wanted.
Now get out the razor -
Applaud your flaws and leave me be.

I'm not here for perfect nails, hair, or perfect bloody tits.

I'm here to make you cry - and heal.

Wake up. That's on you.

I'm here to love.
To be me.
To have fun.
To light up the fucking world -
Just by being me.

I no longer hide.
Even though you tried.
I am strong.
I am wild.
I am a rebel.
And I am free.

KRIS DAVIES

I'M NOT JUST 'ME'

I am not just me
I am not just Mum, Daughter, Sister
I am not just friend, colleague, responsible adult
I am me

I am me in all my fullness
I am the creatrix of all
I channel the magic of the universe
I weave the threads of life and opportunity
I call forward my soul desires into my reality
I choose this

I choose my highest destiny timeline
The one that was pre-written
Exactly for me
Gifts from ancient times, lifetimes and galaxies
Wisdom that has been lived, shared and re-found
Expansion beyond the veiled 3D
Into the higher realms, through love

I accept all that I am
All that I have ever been
All that I am calling in
I accept
For I am me

No longer to be hidden
No longer to be denied
No longer to be forgotten

I step into the awesome power of me
Me in all my possibilities
To claim the beauty and joy aligned to me at birth
I step into me
I accept me
I love myself unconditionally
I have all that I need within me, right at this moment
I am ready
I am complete
I am a New Earth being of light

I am ready to be me
I am me

And so it is

ROMELLA JONES

The Sacred Transformation

I emerge from the darkness,
stronger than before,
co-creating with the Universe,
learning to love myself more,
with passion and flame.
No longer broken,
no longer the same,
yet there is fire in my softness
and grace in my scars;
a love born from stillness,
as deep as the stars.
Each breath is a promise,
each exhale a prayer.
I am the lover
who's always been there.
I rise not for rescue,
nor for someone to claim,
but for the thrill of becoming
my own sacred name.
I have shed all that was heavy,
all that dimmed my own light,
moving on with my life,
bare, bold, and bright.
No longer a shadow
of who I should be,

I am wholly,
wildly,
wonderfully me.

Jane Beverley

That little girl
I hid away
I'm proud of now,
she fought to stay

The Girl I Hid Away

I kept you hidden for so long
Shut the door because you didn't belong
Never letting you look outside
Always feeling you were something to hide

A little girl with so much to say
Too much for others so stay away
I punished you for being true
I didn't want to be like you

You were courage, you held your own
But it got you no-where other than alone
You were not liked instead you were abused
Told you were nothing, your personality refused

So, I locked the door and hid the key
In a place where no one would ever see
The little girl hiding, desperate to get out
Ignored you even when you tried to shout

I locked you away but let others in
Those who pushed me down and would always win
Their voices I held for years of my life

Their negativity sat in my body, so rife

I was ashamed of you for so very long
Told over again that you didn't belong
I should be quiet, seen but not heard
That little girl wouldn't have taken those words

You tried to push back, but my fight was strong
I had been convinced that you were wrong
That I was better, when I wasn't too much
I shouldn't hold on to you as a crutch

I'm so very sorry because now I can see
That little girl was everything me
You deserved the freedom I took away
So now I promise to pave the way

I'll make you proud and you will see
The change will start from within me
I'll no longer hide from the girl you once were
I'll make sure everyone knows about her

Because you were my strength, my power, my guide
I should never have trapped you deep inside
You are worthy of love and should be seen from afar

Because you are like a guiding star

I've thrown away that lock and key
Permission to embrace the whole of me
That little girl I hid away
I'm proud of now, she fought to stay

VERITY CURRYER

Unchained

I never knew what life could be,
conditioned young to not achieve.
My wings clipped short, my chains so tight,
dreams were just a distant sight.

But deep inside a burning grew,
is it so wrong to want it all?
I have a voice, I have a dream,
it's not their fault – I CAN be seen.

I listen to my inner voice,
she loves, she smiles, she encourages choice.
My fire grows, my passion soars,
I can rip down those fucking walls.

I am not the person that they can see,
I am strong and brave with identity.
There is no-one to hold me down,
my chains are broken, my wings returned.

I thought that inner turmoil had kept me small,
Instead it taught me to be bold.
It doesn't matter what others think,
My heart is pure, my intentions sweet.
I stand stripped bare for all to see,

not bothered by those that look at me.
My vision is strong, my mission is clear,
I need to spread my message clear.

You are not weak, you are not small,
conditioning has trapped us all.
Listen to your inner voice,
dream big, love hard, demand it all.

For once we break our shackles and chains,
we reclaim our power, we are free again.
Our spirit soars, our soul ignites,
YOU hold the key, it's in your sight.

SUE QUINNEY

Who is She?

Who is she?
This girl I see,
Those deep, sad eyes looking back at me.

So many thoughts.
So many dreams.
So many wishes, in you I see.

You've come this far,
Yet still you see,
Those deep, sad eyes looking back at me.

Its time to rise up from the sand.
Your heavy heart, wrapped up in bands.
So tightly wrapped, it weighs you down.
Those lines of age, as you frown.

Its time you see,
You and me,
To change those eyes,
Looking back at me.

One step at a time,
Day by day.
Working on loving yourself, your own special way.

Opening up to all you are.
Loving yourself, just as you are.
Today, dear me, what do you see?

I see those eyes looking back at me.
A glimmer of hope,
A moment of joy.

I see the beauty once more in me.

JUSTINE HENDLEY

Sometimes

Sometimes, it's so hard
I've wanted to tell you so many times
I've wanted the best for you
I've wanted all the happiness there is for you

Sometimes, it's so hard
When I was young, I knew it all
No-one could feel as I do
My children, when they come, will have it all -
love and understanding

Sometimes, it's so hard
There is no help, no sympathy when we make
mistakes
It does not matter.
You are loved, you are understood I am your mother
and so very proud of you

Sometimes, it's so hard
I have reached the age of turmoil
I took all the precautions, but still, I start to doubt
Should I have taken a different view?

Sometimes, it's so hard
It cannot be, I know no other way

I have tried to be the mother I wanted - I needed
I could do no more

Sometimes, it's so hard
When you are angry, when you curse
A feeling of panic washes over me
I feel responsible, your pain is my pain and more

Sometimes, it's so hard

Sometimes, it's easy
When I feel you are happy and content
These are the times I feel everything is worthwhile
Thank you, you gave me so much.

June Reason

Full of Cheer

I wake up every morning
Thinking what today will bring
Knowing that I'm happier
Now life is full of cheer

The days are gone when life was bad
Where work and daily life made me sad
Getting through the day was tough
And at the end of each day I'd had enough

Covid - that is it where it all began
My passion for dance had to come to an end
The travelling each week was becoming a struggle
And the dance party business had broken like rubble

The urge to help children with additional needs
Guided me towards education and special needs
Two years later and now a qualified TA
I was head hunted to work within secondary AP

It all started well - I was on top of the world
But then suddenly one day it started to unfold
Meetings to say I was not pulling my weight
And accusing me of not doing things right
Three months went by, I did what I was told

And then just like that I was asked to go

Four months of toing and froing with my union rep
Not feeling right and being signed off with stress
I was scared to leave the house and did not like going out
But knew I had to turn things around

One year on after not knowing what to do, having to sign on
I'm back on track and having fun
I've found a job within the NHS, with a team who are awesome
And a job that I love

KYM GREEN

And when I cede to Source, to flow,
They move in me... and I can glow

We Are The Elements

I walk with Earth beneath my feet,
Where crystal secrets softly sleep.
She holds me close in stone and clay,
And keeps me safe along the way.

The wind that moves through sky and hair,
Is not just breeze, it's silent prayer.
It lifts the thoughts I long to free,
And hums the truth of all I'll be.

The sea can soothe or she can roar,
She calls me in to feel once more.
Her waves reflect what lies below,
The rise, the fall, the letting go.

The fire dances with sheer delight,
It burns away the need to fight.
It warms my hands and stirs my name,
And fills my chest with quiet flame.

The aether calls in space between,
In dreams, in stillness, soft, unseen.
It speaks in pulses, wide and slow
A star borne thread through all I know.
These elements are not just mine,

They stir in ways I cannot know.
And when I cede to Source, to flow,
They move in me… and I can glow.

VICKIE THOMPSON

St George's Daughter: The dragon never needed slaying - she was always me.

I was not rescued by light or luck,
no hand reached down, no spell was cast.
It was just me, breathless and broken,
in the silence after everything had been burned to the ground.

They don't tell you that ruin can be freeing,
that being shattered strips the mask away.
I met myself in the wreckage,
and that version did not flinch one bit from the fire.

There was a death not of body, but of pretending.
A letting go that tasted like gin and salty tears.
Every mask melted, every defence undone,
until only my soul remained, raw and true.

I didn't escape the pain I walked into it.
Not to suffer, but to see.
Somewhere deep down I knew:
there's no becoming without first unbecoming.

I wasn't saving myself from the fire.
I was saving myself through it.

Through every unanswered ache,
and every version of me that didn't quite fit.

No familiar face came to save me.
No miracle softened the edges.
It was my own heartbeat and that inner fighter
that whispered: rise.

And I did.
Not polished, not sure,
but honest,
and that was enough.

I rose barefoot, bloody, aching,
through ashes that still smoked with memory.
My strength was not gifted.
It was grown in the dark, with no witness.

It didn't roar. It hummed.
A quiet defiance. A sacred knowing.
A flame that belonged to no one but me,
and I carried it home in my bones.

I didn't come back the same.
I came back true.
Not the version they could handle
the version I had always been.

I built a new life with trembling hands,
not to prove anything, but to live.
To honour the breath I chose to take

when I could have stayed silent forever.

Now I walk with softness and fire,

with reverence for the dark that taught me.

I am not who I was

and I would not return even if I could.

This strength is mine.

Not borrowed, not begged for.

A bloody, messy, hard-earned truth

etched into the fabric of my being.

I am not what was done to me.

I am what I did with it.

A woman reborn by her own hands,

beautiful, unshakeable, and free.

And maybe it was written from the start

born on St George's Day, dragon-born, headline
bold.

Not here to be saved,

but to rise in full view of the world.

They called me fierce before I had language.

They watched me appear, minutes old, already seen.

And now I remember why:

I was never meant to hide.

JOHANNE STIMSON

I WILL HOLD YOU IN MY HEART

In memory of Ernest Marsh

I will hold you in my heart
Whilst you create the light that guides me on the path out of the dark.
Grief is such an individual journey
No step or process can be skipped
You will have to return to the pain and hurt at later date.
I feel grateful for having you heal my heart.
So, I guess that is why, I feel such deep sadness that you are, no longer in the physical plane, and we had to part.
Yet the love we shared does not disappear into the air
It is ignited and the flames becomes brighter the more I say your name.
Even though I know things will never been the same.
Remembering the good memories, being the wise ones who celebrate those we love who have passed.
The laughter, the love, the connection of a soul light
I am proud to be your daughter, as you will always my spiritual father.
You held me when the tears fell, I knew I could tell you anything.
A special light, energy a healing source of love

without judgement.
You are the 'physical' light I miss, yet I know I hold you deep within my heart, my mind, my soul
That energy will never fade or grow old.
Lucky to have had you in my life for 21 years
Fortunate to have you now, within my spiritual family.
Strengthening that intuitive transformational connection,
Guiding me, protecting me and to be all that I can BE.
Creating the space where inner healing can take place.
I am all of this because you Loved Me.
I will always hold you in my heart, so we are never really apart.

From your loving Daughter Diana

DIANA E TYSON

A PROMISE TO HERSELF,
SHE SAID, WITH A LITTLE FIRE...
PERFECT VISION IS THE QUEST.

OH YES, OH YES, OH YES!

SURVIVAL

I'm stood on a line.
As thin as a strand of hair, as sharp as a single blade.

It runs beneath me and splits me in two.
Cuts down from my skull, exactly through the
tumour that sits behind my eyes.

I live on it.
No - I survive on it.
The line etched deep into me.

They say your twenties are for living fast,
for freedom, and foolish choices.
Mine are between hospitals and silent screams.
My rebellion? Survival.

I balance on this line every moment.
In a body, brain, and mind that resist me.

Panicking over wasted time,
Yet grateful to just be alive.
Never feeling I'm doing enough to show that,
As I obsess over an end that may - or may not - be
near.

There's no way of knowing.
So I'm a girl in her twenties relying on one given: the line.

I don't want it to define me.
So a persona rises.
She protects me, from me.
She stands on big stages. Tells big stories.
She makes real change.

This sharp line has carved into me.
But in her skin, it finds a place to be.

When I'm me.
No one hears how loud I scream.
Trying so very hard to show I'm capable.
Carrying the weight of existing in their world.
A world I'll never feel I should be in.

Maybe it's the line cutting through my voice box.

When I leave this line it's my definitive end.
So whilst I'm here the pain from these lines ingraining into my body: those screams are calls to power for change.

I can't do it.

But she can.
Deep down, she is me.
She won't let this line define me.

MOLLY FENTON

Detached

Just another day, going with the flow.
Then all of a sudden, the clouds appear and blow me,
to and fro.
Oh no, oh no, oh no.

There's something very wrong, I think.
My eyes, they're not quite right. What's wrong with
my sight?
Fright, fright, fright.

It's off for tests and scans, back in NHS land. But I
already know what they will say.
It's happening once again.

No time to digest, bypass A and E, no money for
passing Go.
It's emergency surgery all the way.
Go, go, go!

24 hours of madness, of blackness beyond compare.
Such terror and vulnerability, flayed open for all to
share.
My light has dimmed to naught. I don't know where
I am.

My place in the world has vanished, how easily it
can.

Delving into the deep abyss, dragged down with
panic and fear.
What if this is all there is, my dear?
Living in the fear.

If blindness comes knocking on my door once more,
what do I do now?
What am I good for, if all is dark?
How, how, how?

But then glimmers of light appear like stars
twinkling through the sky.

The blue and white of that uniform, a sight for my
sore eye.
A sigh of relief, and a curse: thank fuck, for God is
here with luck, luck, luck.

This is just the start of this healing tale.
There will be more tears, upset and pain.
Come play with us in the dark once more.
Life from technicolour to muted grey.
Oh no, oh no, oh no.

The things I took for granted, currently out of reach.
Nipping to the shops alone, not safe for me, I think.
For oil protects what was detached, obscuring all
around.

'To rest, to rest, to rest', they say.
But keep the blackness far away.

But just beyond the horizon, a rising force once more.
Hope and a quiet, determined strength come
knocking at my door.
A siren call, a vow within, to do my best and more.
Positivity all the way is the quiet roar.

A promise to herself, she said, with a little fire…
Perfect vision is the quest.

Oh yes, oh yes, oh yes!

RACHAEL BRODIE

Kindness Waits

Kindness is not a weakness.
It is the quiet force that keeps us human.

It does not shout for attention.
It notices.
The tired eyes in a meeting.
The pause in a friend's voice.
The weight someone is carrying
but cannot name.

Kindness waits.
It makes space.
It says: you first
and means it.

We have learned to rush,
to measure worth in what we finish,
to guard ourselves against being taken for granted.
And in the process
We forget the art of being gentle
- with each other,
with ourselves.

True kindness is not just what we give away.
It is what we allow ourselves to receive.

The permission to rest.
The grace to begin again.
The courage to meet our own reflection
without judgement.

Imagine if we made kindness our default.
Not as performance,
not as a strategy,
but as the air we breathe.

The world would soften.
And so would we.

ANDREA RAINSFORD

Learnings

In the realm of knowledge, a splendid domain,
Where minds are nurtured, like trees in rain,
Let me weave a poem, a tale to be told,
Of the wonders that await, when curiosity unfolds.

Step into the classroom, a world so vast,
Where curiosity thrives, and dreams are amassed,
With each passing day, new lessons take flight,
Igniting a spark, to illuminate the learning flight.

Learning forms friendships, bonds are formed,
Kindred spirits united, hearts warmed,
Through laughter and chatter, connections bloom,
Lifelong companions, dispelling gloom.

Teaching guides us, as wisdom is shared,
With passion and patience, our guides truly care,
Unlocking the doors to endless possibilities,
Empowering minds and shaping destinies.

But it's not only in school, where learning is found,
Walls of the world the only boundary held,
Each need is different, just like our brains,
Meeting what's needed moves the learning train.

In the realm of discovery, wonders unfold,
Science, art, and stories yet untold,
From the galaxies above to the depths of the sea,
A treasure trove of knowledge for you and for me.

Challenges arise, no obstacles to fear,
Resilience is nurtured, with compassion and care,
With every setback, a chance to learn and grow,
To rise above, with determination's glow.

In the realm of curiosity, dreams take flight,
Skills honed, talents shining bright,
From library, stage or sports field, all are embraced,
They're all stages for greatness, life's canvas of grace.

So, embrace the journey, with each new day,
Embrace the lessons that come your way,
For in the realm of learning, therein lies the key,
To unlock a future, bright and free.

Let's cherish the positives, that learning bestows,
As we embark on a path where knowledge flows,
For in the halls of learning, hearts are refined,
And a world of possibilities, we shall find.

Learning can be what you make it to be,
It is not set in stone nor should be governed by

powers that be,
It is where your heart takes you, especially when ADHD,
Interest learning calms your soul and will take you to where you want to be.

Sharon Templeman

Let Love

Let love be your anchor,
Let love be your compass
Let love be your destiny and your journey

Let love in and let love out
Let love be your friend and help you understand
your foe

Let love be your protector
Let love keep you strong and help you weather any
storm

Let love be your companion
Let love be your guide
For you are love and love will always bring you
home

Geraldine Crane

Letter to a Younger Me

The strength you always wished you had, is what keeps you upright and moving forward, when the world is a battering ram on your senses.
The confidence you always wished you had, is the ready smile to a stranger, the nod of a head and the way you always give compliments when you like someone's outfit or the way they wear their hair.
You don't see how strong you are because you're struggling through each day, but when you get through this and look back, you'll see that many would have given up long before.
You don't see how confident you are, because confidence is not about putting that bikini on and walking round like you own the world, it's putting that bikini on in the first place.
That courage you always wished you had, is the reason this 'poem' exists.
You don't see how brave you are because you're just too busy getting on with it. You do what has to be done, whatever it takes, because that's who you are.
You stood up in a room full of people and spoke with passion about something you hold dear.
Nobody saw how scared you were, because you paused, you took a breath and you owned it.

If you could see what I see you'd never doubt yourself. If you could see what I see, you'd rule the world.
These days of doubt seem long and drawn, but they were over in a flash. It's time now, you are ready to be seen.

You are the brightest star in the sky
You are the moon in all her glory
You hold the goddess within you
Shine my precious love.

NINA WARREN

You always rise,
even with trembling hands

Life is a Rollercoaster

Life can be kind yet cruel.
It gives with one hand and takes with the other.
You start to relax,
to celebrate,
Only to be hit harder than imagined.

As you slowly breathe again,
You find…
you can't breathe at all.
That ache in your chest,
the silence that screams,
the weight of uncertainty pressing down.

Why?
You whisper to the stars,
the moon,
the sky,
But the answers never feel enough.
You ask the same questions,
Not wanting answers,
just a break.

A moment where life doesn't feel like a hostage.
Hoping, praying, begging that this time,
all will be okay.

Dreams on hold.
Life in limbo.
The future foggy.
The present fragile.
And yet,
you know you can cope.
You did last time.
You will again.
You always rise, even with trembling hands.

Support surrounds you,
Loving arms,
kind words,
gentle souls.
But still, moments feel lonely,
Like screaming in a crowded room.

Life is a rollercoaster,
Not one you choose,
But one you hold onto, with all you've got.

And even in this storm,
Somewhere deep within,
There is a spark,
a sacred knowing...
You are stronger than sorrow.
Love will carry you.

Light will return.

Maybe not today,
But it will…
And when it does,
So will your breath,
Your peace,
Your dreams.

ZOE NEWTH

Ffynone

Light reaches the cliff before I do,
It moves across the rock slowly, certain.

Fynone is already awake.
Water tumbles without hesitation,
A ribbon of sound in a quiet, soft place.

I step into the pool below.
Cold at first,
Then something else,
a welcome.

Sunlight touches the surface.
And the water answers,
with a shimmer,
that slips across my shoulders,
tracing my spine, holding me.

Haze rises, the air holds gold.
For a moment,
I float.
Weightless.
Wordless.
Part of the morning, part of everything.

Clare Fentham

Love

love
this well spring of emotion lifts you up like the tides of the ocean

love
this simple gift of a hug and a kiss warms you up inside like total bliss

love
the small little word
sometimes has you acting a little absurd

love
this heart lead feeling often has you reeling

love
this big emotion is meant for us all
as we accept the heaviness will fall

Heather and Mateah (age 7)

LOVE IS...

Did you get home?
Did you eat?
How can I help?
Can we meet?

I thought of you,
I saved you this.
It exists everywhere,
Not just a kiss.

It's folded clothes,
and favourite foods.
It's all around,
In all your moods.

It's washing dishes,
Box set bingeing.
Dancing in the kitchen,
Random singing.

Its not on Facebook,
Or Instagram friendly.
We're not tiktok famous,
As Love isn't always -trendy,

It's *I'm sorry I shouted,*
Sorry I'm late.
It's carrying each other,
Not just your soul mate.

Love can be family,
It reaches for miles.
Love is that moment,
Where one of you smiles.

If we all put Love first,
I'm 100% certain.
No wars, or drugs,
No one is a burden.

We have all been hurt,
Even wore a broken heart,
But love is the way,
Right from the start.

I know it sounds soppy,
I've been lost too.
I'm so grateful for Love,
I love you too.

KIKI

MY DARLING, YOU ARE MAGIC

My Darling, you are MAGIC
And you don't have a clue
The way that you light up the world
Just by being you

My Darling, you are POWERFUL
In ways you cannot see
But know and trust that one day soon
You'll see all you are meant to be

My Darling, you are FEARLESS
Each day you go all in
You give everything you have to life
You are always going to win

My Darling, you are FIRE
Your passion speaks so loud
To all the souls that cross your path
You make me feel so proud

My Darling, you are WISDOM
Beyond your tender years
The way you give to everyone
And melt away their fears
My Darling, you are LOVE itself

In all you say and do
Your laughter is angelic
Your heart is just so true

My Darling, you are PERFECT
Please don't change a thing
Keep spreading love out in the world
And watch the joy you bring

My Darling, you are PRECIOUS
A gift from up above
You have completely changed my life
With nothing but your love.

LOUISE GREEN

For the Days You Forget Your Magic

My girls, my loves, there's so much to say,
I hope my words make sense one day,
Right now, you are young and are going through,
Changes that will one day empower you.

Your voice can be loud, your body tensed up,
But never feel like you're ever too much,
Your shouting, your anger, your laughter too,
Is welcome here, it's what makes you, you.

As you grow older you may doubt your worth,
You may even feel you don't matter or worse,
But listen when I tell you, your impact is real,
You are perfect, you matter, you're the real deal.

You'll be tempted to people please just to feel loved,
You deserve better than that, these thoughts should be shoved,
If people don't love you for just who you are,
They're not your people because you are a star.

Speak to yourself kindly, your words impact your mind,
Don't be tempted to say things that feel unkind,
You influence yourself more than others will,
Be good to yourself, that doesn't take skill.

If someone ever says you are too sensitive,
Take it as a compliment because I promise it is,
Sensitivity is strength, it's compassion and love,
Don't ever feel you need to rise above.

Your feelings matter, don't let them be quashed,
Don't push things down or make them squashed,
Big feelings are good, let them out, let them roar,
If others don't like it, show them the door.

Culture will tell you should be busy all the time,
Have it together, never break down or cry,
But beautiful girls, self-love is a must,
Rest when it's needed, you're worth so much fuss.

If others don't like it, that's on them not on you,
Never do something you don't want to do,
Listen to your gut, you know yourself well,
If it doesn't feel right, it's ok to yell.

Joy is your birthright, happiness is free,
Don't deny yourself sunshine, be all you can be,
Don't let anyone else ever dim your light,
Shine my darlings, so very bright.

VERITY CURRYER

Look at us closely
and you'll see what I mean
When I tell you that
not all witches are green

I've lost my Mum

No one understands, I've just lost my Mum
It's hard to talk to anyone
It's a struggle every day, just to get out of bed
With all the sad thoughts inside my head

No one understands - I've just lost my Mum
It's hard to think straight or get the washing done
It's like a nightmare that I can't wake up from
Every minute, every hour, every day - Missing my Mum

Don't you understand?! I've just lost my Mum
I'm expected to go back to normal and look after everyone
I can't even look after myself right now
But I'm supposed to carry on, as normal, somehow

Don't you understand? I've just lost my Mum
That's why I'm crying, I'm angry, and I can't seem to have fun
She ripped out a part of me when she left this earth
She took a piece of my soul to be with hers

No one understands. I just want to be alone
I don't want to meet up, I want to stay at home

I want to curl up into a ball and stay in bed all day
I miss my Mum so much. But - what would my
Mum say?!

She'd say *I love you, Annie, babe, but please don't cry*
Remember your what, how, when, who, and why
Show your children that when you lose someone
Your love never ends, but your life can carry on

Make peace with your woes and always remember to be kind
Especially to yourself, work out your body and your mind
Babe, now it's your time to show everyone what you do
Your artistic talent is a magical gift, unique to you

Keep writing, keep sharing, keep doodling and painting
This is the moment of your life that we've all been waiting!
....Ok Mum, that's what I'll do, I'll make you proud
I'm going to make a difference in this world and stand out from the crowd

I'm gonna help others who've suffered like us
Who just can't get off that spiralling down bus
I'm gonna end mental health waiting lists
I'm gonna design youth centres that the kids can't resist

And when my message has spread all over the world,
I hope you'll be proud of me, Mum? Because I'll
always be proud to be your little girl.

ANNIE HUNT

Not all Witches are green

Neither are we the 'wicked witch of the west'
We are the women who stand up and are seen
To use our voices to say no
When others are coerced to say yes

We are the women who can't ignore
Who rise up together and say 'no more'
We are the women who 'they' try to silence
The ones whose opinions they tell us are wrong
We are the women who smile and stay strong

Because we know our opinions come from our values
And our values are calling us to stand where we belong
We are the women who speak the words others are thinking
Who give voice to the others with passion and grace
Knowing our words will be thrown back in our face

We are the women who continue to rise
Knowing our numbers are growing in size
We are the women who'll lift you and hold you
Even when others are trying to stop us

Just know we are here, we've stood up for ourselves
And we'll keep standing up and we'll keep giving voice
To what you are thinking till you make your choice
We'll be here beside you when you choose to say no
To stand up for yourself, to stand up and to grow

We're all around you, we're women you know
We're your friends, your sisters, your mothers and aunts
We're not weird or eccentric, we're women like you
We've chosen to say enough is enough
You no longer get to treat us this way

Look at us closely and you'll see what I mean
When I tell you that not all witches are green.

JAN OCKENDON

Not Defined By Numbers

I'm not defined by numbers,
Not the dress size, date, or scale.
Not the candles on my birthday cake,
Or the relationships that failed.

I've earned each line upon my face,
Each silver streak I wear.
They're trophies of the life I've led,
Not flaws I must repair.

I've lived a life of colour,
Climbed hills and danced on bars.
I've loved and lost, then loved again,
And learned to heal my scars.

I've chased my dreams, I've changed my mind,
I've started late and loud.
I've failed, I've flourished, I've broken rules,
And frankly, I'm quite proud.

So keep your labels and your tags,
And lack of liberty.
I'm not defined by numbers,
I'm a soul who's been set free!

Lorna Griffiths

Beyond the Broken

Now covered in lines, each bearing the memories of my life,
I glance down to reminisce through the postcards of my life.
I remember the vibrant girl, who refused to be beaten into submission,
The one that was fiery and refused to ask for permission.

The girl who danced wildly in the rain,
And lived through book characters to escape the pain.
Fast forward, that carefree girl grew into a determined young adult,
Who challenged the norm, beat the rules, and claimed her right to vote.
She thought she was on top, that no one could bring her down.

Until her parents decided to move towns.
In an instant, she lost her footing, her confidence, her place.
Her world turned upside down, she couldn't find grace.
It began with anxiety, then depression took hold,

She masked it with anger, fear, and stories untold.
She clung to the little voice in her head,
Whispering life was against her, something to dread.
She reasoned that voice was only keeping her safe,
So she pulled away, hid her pain, kept the faith.
Through adulthood, she silently screamed into the void:
'Why am I here? What's left to enjoy?
Isn't it the fittest, the strongest, who survive?
I've exhausted my worth, I'm barely alive.'

These thoughts plagued her days, haunted her nights,
Until she slowed down and let in the light.
She reconnected with herself, rekindled her spark,
And found the girl who once danced in the dark.
She opened her heart, filled it with ambition.

Poured joy into life, ignited her mission.
Unbridled, daring, with mischief in her eyes,
She re-established her worth, realised she was the prize.
By loving herself, she became an example to follow,
No more shrinking, no more expectations to swallow.

She shone from within, meant for this Earth,
Her light inspired others to claim their own worth.

'To help every woman in the world heal,' she vowed,

Her passion became her mission, her voice strong
and loud.
One woman at a time, she helped them climb,
Summiting mountains, releasing old binds.
Now as she glances at the mirror, lines gracing her
face,
She remembers her impact, her grit, her grace.
A life devoted to helping women reclaim their song,
To love themselves deeply, where they truly belong.

RACHEL COUDRON

Please find the courage
To follow your star
Lead from your heart
Show us who you are

One More Day

On Boxing Day, you drifted away,
I always hoped you were here to stay,
The world feels dimmer, since you were called away,
If only we had just one more day.

A lorry man, the road & convoy your song,
Through endless miles, you drove along,
Your truck was your pride, your second home,
Kindness marked where you would roam.

A mountain road, the Alps so high,
You turned around, without asking why,
To help a stranger stranded there,
That's who you were, a heart so rare.

At home, your laughter filled the air,
Watching darts, Formula One & constructing Lego
with care,
Piece by piece, you'd build it with pride,
Joy and patience side by side.

A cheeky smile, so many stories you told,
A warmth that never could grow old,
From stranger's glance, to friend so fast,
You had a gift that few on earth could grasp.

But most of all, for us, your two,
You were our rock, our guide so true.
For Mum, for us, and your 3 grandchildren too,
Your love was endless, through and through.

Dad, you taught us work, you taught us play,
You showed us love in every way.
And now our hearts break and sway,
What we'd give for just, one more day.

DAWN EVANS

Ripples of Love

Epicentral beauty,
I feel your glow.
Sweetly whispering,
You ebb and you flow.

Wondrous nature,
Guides me on.
From where I've been,
Past all who've gone.

Silently held in pure loving light,
Gently supported each day and each night.
Deepest roots grow crystal clear,
Grounding me infinitely, always here.

Phoenix embers roll with glee,
Opening their pathways fully back to me.
Loving butterfly wings,
Brush my cheeks.

Dragon breath,
Lifts me moonbeam high.
Cascading waterfall,
Ruffles my tears.

Rejoicing each lesson,
Peeling back the years.
'You've made it my love!',
She twinkles aloud.

Look at all you've created,
Connected around.
For all that you are,
For everywhere you've been.

Hidden, forgotten, serving unseen,
Now my sweet dearest it's your time to shine.
Skip, slip out of your cocoon,
Radiate through the wide open skies.

All timelines drift,
They each fall away.
For this beloved is your rebirth,
Today.

With so much love, light, and gratitude for you
Exactly as you are now and always.

LIZ CLIFTON

RISE

You feel the shift
You feel the wave
You hear the call
Now just be brave

Deep breath in
Deep breath out
Trust the process
Ignore the doubt

Its time to move
Its time to stand
Head held high
We're holding your hand

One step forward
And again
You have got this
Its about to begin

You are rising
Up above
To shine your light
And share your love

Your soul is calling
Your heart is free
You are rising
For all to see

The time is now
You're not behind
Creating ripples
For all mankind

Angels are calling
The Universe too
Step up to the plate
Authentically you

People are waiting
For the words that you say
For they are so needed
In every way

Please find the courage
To follow your star
Lead from your heart
Show us who you are

You are loved beyond measure
Just know like you know

This is your purpose
It is time to go

You are fully supported
In every way
Step forth, dear Sister
You're starting today

The signs are around
The whispers are loud
Trust in the guidance
And make yourself proud

Your dreams have been calling
Now you begin
Follow the breadcrumbs
Connect deep within

Forget all the questions
Just quieten down
Know that you've got this
And straighten your crown

Your tribe are ready
For all that you are
You're going to smash it
You are meant to go far

No more excuses
No time to wait
Your prayers have been answered
Today is the date

For all your desires
Your dreams coming true
The magic is moving
Especially for you

Recall your power
Look straight ahead
Remember your calling
And what your soul said

Roll the tape forward
To a year from today
The first time you showed up
To say what you say

And now you have made it
The life you desire
You rose like a Goddess
And followed your fire

LOUISE GREEN

ROSE-TINTED

'A wheelchair by Christmas' they said.
They must be wrong, I'm healthy, the thoughts ran through my head!
I'm in my twenties. I have a little man. *What did I do wrong? This isn't my plan.*
Years went by, injections, infusions. I did as I was told.
I wasn't disabled I didn't fit into this mould.
I slowly got worse and my legs wouldn't play.
It's about to happen, it'll be any day.
No I said pulling up my big girl pants, *I'm not willing to give up,* and then I took a stance.
A new treatment, a bought of chemo… to Russia it would be.
I left my hair, waistline and MS in Moscow. I shouted out, so everyone would know.
A chronic illness may try and make the body or even mind stinted, but with a huge smile on your face you can keep your life Rose-tinted.
A DIAGNOSIS IS NOT A FULL STOP.
With honesty I've found my power, now help me, to the roof top!

KEZIA KECIBAS

Sacred Space

It isn't a stone circle, yet it could be
It isn't a church or a temple, although possibly
It isn't a gathering of souls, but it can be
It isn't Glastonbury, Chalice Wells the Springs or the Tor, not only
It isn't outside of you

It is within you
It is around you
It is your space
It is your creation
It is your energy
It is how you show up

You may add to the external locations
Feel their vibrations and frequencies adding to your own inner vibration
Expanding your inner connection, your connection to source and beyond
It is all you

It is through self-awareness of your E- motions, your energy in motion and stillness
It is through your attention, focus and desires
It is through your quiet inner voice, your existence

It is through your self-love, appreciation and self-worth
It is through your prioritising yourself, your needs and practises
It is through believing you are worthy of all
It is through receiving the gifts with a grateful heart
It is through showing up as your wholeness, with your vulnerabilities, your desires
It is showing up for yourself in a physical, mental, emotional and spiritual level when it counts
It is coming home to you

It is all within you
You don't need crystals, candles, altars or props
They may add to your intention
They may support your energy
The truth is you are sacred space, you always were, you always will be

Find your sacred space in your being, not your doing

You are loved, you are worthy, you are sacred
You are the sacred space you search for
Guide yourself in
Through your presence, your thoughts, your energy, your groundedness, through love
And radiate this around you

You are the sacred space you search for externally

You are home
You are sacred space
We need no more

I am sacred space

And so it is

ROMELLA JONES

Shadow Dance

On the beach, in the play park
Shadows of ones that might have been
A younger boy, an older girl
The hidden siblings who'll never be seen

My daughter, as yet, does not know
Of the crew that might've been right there
Holiday buddies, secrets aplenty
When times got rough, special souls to care

As the landscape of life rises and falls
A support team on hand, come what may
To laugh, to cry, to hug, to scream
Should we become frail and pass away

It's often asked 'is she the only one?'
She's my one and only. If that's the same.
Amongst the shadows, she dances through life
Lighting up mine, since the day she came.

And I'll give all my strength to bolster hers
Should she need extra to manage alone
And I know somehow the babes that were lost
In our hearts - and the shadows - will always be
known.

Andrea Byrne

SHE SOARS WITH THE VOICES
OF THE FEW
AND OF THE MANY

She Builds

She stands at the edge where the brave begin,
Not with fear, but fire within.
No script to follow, no guiding hand,
Just dreams and grit, a quiet stand.

She draws her plans on sleepless nights,
Fuelled by hope and stubborn fights.
Her courage sips from morning's brew,
Each task a brick in something new.

No doors flung wide, no grand parade,
Just steps she takes and dues she's paid.
She speaks her worth, no longer small,
A voice once soft now stands tall.

They might not see the seeds she sows,
Or how her quiet power grows.
They miss the grace in staying true,
In doing what she has to do.

There are days the doubt runs deep,
When dreams are hard to hold or keep.
But still she shows up, rain or shine,
And claims the space she knows is mine.

She dreams, yes - but she builds, too,
With steady hands and vision true.
No map to show the way ahead,
Just trust in every step she's led.

Each setback builds the frame she needs,
Each scar a line her strength now reads.
With faith she lays foundation stone,
And builds her dream from dreams she's sown.

One day she'll turn and clearly see,
The woman she had dared to be.
And smile at all the roads she braved,
The life she dreamed - the life she made.

Angela L Powell

BRANCHES FROM THE ANCIENT TREE

She doesn't lead with noise,
But with presence.
Her power isn't loud.
Its rooted in the soil

Whispered through the trees,
In the breeze, shimmering the leaves.
Her power is wild, yet gentle,
Fed from her soul, nourished by the land.

Her strength is like the wind,
A fierce hug, unyielding.
A whirlwind, twirling.
Lifting the sorrow, spinning it to smiles.

Her resilience is like the hill side rocks,
weathered and worn through the years.
Her compassion like the moss blanket.
Wrapped around you. Whispering... *let go.*

With her the trees lean in when you dance.
With her WE move to the rebel beat,
Made by hooved feet,

The ancestral heartbeats.

I am she. You are she.
We are she.
Branches from the same ancient tree.
We become one.

LISA WARREN

Reclaiming Her Self

She gave her time, to those needing care
And left her own cupboard, empty and bare
She gave her energy, heart and soul
Took tiny steps forward, towards her goals

She gave her all, day in and day out
Not just at home, or work, but when out and about
She gave her everything, to all who mattered
Whilst leaving herself, in pieces, shattered

Not just physically, but mentally too
Cos that's just what, us women do
Plod on, plough through, there's no time to rest
Keep going, keep giving, and do your best

She's taking a minute, to give to her self
Putting everything else, up on the shelf
For if she keeps giving, she'll stumble and fall
With nothing to give, nothing at all

With nothing to give, what else can she do
For those that she loves, for me and for you?
What else can she say, who else can she be
When her soul calls out, *what about me?*

When her soul whispers gently, *it's ok to slow down*
Take a deep breath, and straighten your crown
For you're not just a mama, who's tired or teary
Or a woman who's feeling, worn out and weary

You're so much more, you're a warrior, a queen
And it's time to stand tall, be heard, and be seen
For the world needs you, in all of your glory
So clear your throat, and tell your story

The story that's shaped, your life thus far
Of who you were, and who you are
Of who you're becoming, and who you will be
When you've remembered your truth, and set yourself free

KAREN COLQUHOUN

She Remembered

She remembered the sound of her inner voice,
and she was born again.
It whispered one day, softly:
you are enough.

It whispered like the wind blowing gently,
carrying the feeling of peace and acceptance.
It whispered so quietly at first,
she nearly didn't hear it.

She remembered the sound of her inner voice,
as it grew louder,
as the wind picked up,
and whispered louder to her.

She remembered the sound of her inner voice,
as it grew louder again,
echoing inside,
louder than her tears and pain.

She remembered the sound of her inner voice,
more than a whisper now,
like the dawn chorus singing:
you are enough, you are worthy.

She remembered the sound of her inner voice,
as the whispers changed,
to unmistakable voices and chants:
you are enough.

She remembered the sound of her inner voice,
as the fire in her stomach started to burn again,
as the warrior inside began to wake.

She remembered the sound of her inner voice,
you are enough,
as the words began to ring out loud,
rising up like a storm.

She remembered the sound of her inner voice,
as the light came back in her eyes,
and the passion began to return.

She remembered the sound of her inner voice,
as the fog cleared,
and the sun shone bright.

She remembered the warrior within.
She was enough.
Just as she was.

AMY MOSTERT

SHE...

She is not the story of her season's past, she is the now, the ebb and flow of life and synchronicity

She weaves her magic on the essence of whispers
An all-seeing all-knowing beauty of what will be and what was

The movement of breath and light, her place is given, her place is all and nothing but a sigh of what is to come
Her movement echoes over eons of birth and rebirth, of love and loss

She is the well, the water, the earth, the breeze, the rustle of leaves, the speckles of light on dewy lawns, lakes, and starlit skies

She bows to no one, she is all she needs to be in the now, this moment, this life

Her steps creating imprints of times beyond the veil, steps of existence, steps of motion, of infinity, she knows her path on this earth, in this timeline she is finite

Her steps ripple, ancestor to ancestor, atom to atom, skin to skin

She is love, the light, the shadows, the reason everything exists, the wish that never was, the wish that is, that flows endlessly on the roads less travelled

She holds the weight, the burden, the heaviness, the all-encompassing pressure of what will be, what was, and was never meant to be

She is the colour, the transparency, the mirror, the shadow, the light, the spoken word, the unspoken thought

She releases her essence, her guidance, her wisdom, it echoes, rises on every breath and sigh

She soars with the voices of the few and of the many

She is she, soul to soul...

ANDREA MELLON

Shine Your True Light

There is a gentle glow within you,
Fine as morning's first light,
A quiet gentleness that whispers,
Of the tenderness so bright.

It does not need to shout or force,
The luminous gift you hold,
Like candlelight in windows,
Or dewdrops touched with gold.

Your true light is in your laughter,
The kindness in your eyes,
The way you listen closely,
When a friend begins to cry.

It sparkles as you wonder,
At simple, lovely things,
The warmth you give so freely,
The joy your presence brings.

Sometimes you might forget it,
This radiance you possess,
And ponder if you matter,
If you are enough, no less.

But look how flowers open,
Without a sound or fuss,
How moonbeams paint the water,
With silver, luminous.

Your light is just as precious,
As natural and as true,
A legacy of love and care,
That still shines through to you.

So let it flicker softly,
This beacon in your heart,
A gift passed down through memory,
A light that will not part.

The world needs constant glowing,
Quiet strength and grace,
Your tender light reminds us,
That love lives in every space.

Trust the glow within you,
Let it shine, however small,
For in your gentle radiance,
Others find light for all.

NATALIE TRICE

Some souls create ripples,
too vast to explain,
Magnetic with passion,
yet touched by life's pain.

Sometimes

Sometimes true life just doesn't seem fair and no amount of meditation or journaling, can change the view out there.

Sometimes people are cruel and unkind, they laugh and they judge, they don't look behind.

Sometimes the bullies in schools and in work, make people feel miserable and they simply just smirk.

Sometimes the rich, make decisions each hour, forgetting the poor and needy, as they they decide from their high tower.

Sometimes women are beaten and bruised, for simply being, what they thought others would choose.

Sometimes our animals are taken so quickly, breaking our hearts and making us feel sickly.

Sometimes this world, isn't a fair place, some have soo much and others soo little, yet people are judged and sometimes belittled.

Sometimes people get killed for the colour of their skin, for loving differently, you can't always win.

Sometimes we stare in the mirror and see things we don't like, despite all the compliments, it's just out of sight.

Sometimes we try to lift up our chin, while life can just crumble and we can't look within.

Sometimes those we love are taken so soon, with no understanding, just sadness and gloom.

Sometimes we just want to swear and really not care, as the sadness overwhelms and we feel such despair.

Just Sometimes.

THERESA LE-COUNT

Stardust in the Ripples

'For every soul we've loved and lost
may their ripple live on in us.'

This beautiful soul has gone too soon
And as we sit in silence, we gaze at the moon
Why does it ache, when love runs so deep?
Why do the stars sometimes lull us to sleep?

Yet under the sorrow, love softly glows
It rises around us, above us, it knows.
This soul was rare, radiant, and kind
A spark in the dark, a brilliant mind.

We'll never forget the minutes or years
The laughter, the mischief, the joy, and the tears.
We felt their excitement, their zest for the ride
How they rose through the shadows, with love as their guide.

Some souls create ripples, too vast to explain
Magnetic with passion, yet touched by life's pain.
Some are called early, too soon for our hearts
As babies, as children, before their new starts.

In our humanness, we ask the same why

But stars don't explain when they fall from the sky.
We're all on a journey, a soul-timed plan
No one can know where it ends or began.

So live with intention, feel all you feel
Let the waves crash, healing is real.
And when you've wept, pause and recall
They're never truly gone at all.

They were so special
So bright.
So divine
That Spirit said softly,
'Your mission's done. It's time.'

So now we grieve
We ache, we sing.
Because the echo of love
Is a sacred thing.

Speak their name forever, out loud
Let their ripple remind you
Love like that never truly leaves.

KATIE CAREY

Starseed: Born of Stars

If I let you look, just glimpse inside my head,
You'd see a world of such strange things and words
I've never said.
You'd think I was a nutcase, if I let you in for long,
You'd look around in wonder and think 'What the
hell went wrong?'

A kaleidoscope of colours burst, blocking out the
world,
It moved me to another place, a place where I was
heard.
I was shown the wonder, the glory and the peace,
The auras abound everywhere, and never seemed to
cease.

I was marked as different, damaged, not as good,
Though I have seen the glory and I'd share it if I
could.

I don't see the world as you do, as a finite thing and
fixed,
I see the world as I do, and my thoughts on that are
mixed.
You see I can't explain it, and my thoughts on this
are strong,

I was born here and I live here, but this is not where I belong.

You see I am a starseed, a bringer of the light,
I have often lived in darkness, so you see me shining bright.
I am timeless and I'm ancient, I am young and innocent,
I know myself as love, I am heaven sent.

I was sent to bring you home, to guide you on your way,
To shelter you from darkness, each and every day.
You see I am a starseed, a bringer of the light,
And now there is no darkness, because I shine so bright.

NINA WARREN

Storm Born

In my head, where storms still swirl,
I cling to hope like a battle call.
Each breath becomes my rhythm tight,
I hold on hard through darkest night.

I bend, don't break. I rise, don't hide.
I am the storm I've walked beside.

Adversity paints in colours stark,
Each wound a line, each scar a mark.
I bloom in soil, soaked through with pain,
Learning to swim, in falling rain.

Change sweeps in like a tide unkind,
Reshaping thought, unhooking mind.
I've shed old skins, revealed what's true;
From shattered roots, I rise anew.

I bloomed through cracks they paved with rules,
Rewrote the book, reclaimed my tools.
No neat endings, no tidy lines,
Just healing loud, in tangled rhymes.

So here I am; no veil, no script.
No shame inside, this skin I've gripped.

Not brave. Not fixed. Just fully lit.
Unashamed, and refusing to quit.

Softness comes like spring through ice,
A quiet bloom, a breath concise.
I hear the hush, my heart's own song…
And find I've carried peace all along.

Storm-born, soul-lit, I stand here firm,
Unapologetically authentic, rebuilt, reborn.

MAGGIE CEE

That Woman Is Me

I knew a woman, years ago: she was barely more than a child,
yet burdened with bruises far older than her bones.
An old soul, new only to herself.

Life had carved harsh lessons into the marrow of her hope.
Beaten down, not just by fists,
but by the endless ache of being unseen,
It was no surprise when she reached for another.

She believed. She trusted.
Grateful her eyes weren't yet open.

She wore kindness like a coat, but underneath,
a silence sharp enough to bleed.
No blows, just black velvet wounds,
that no one else could see.

They said he was wonderful, too good for her.
How little they knew, their hurtful words would wound some more.
They didn't see,
the rooms she cried in, the words unsaid, that stung more than any scream.

Still, she loved.
She forgave.
Her nature: soft as mist,
strong as stone.

Years passed by, and now she sits in winter,
her silver strands where fire once lived,
energy faded, but never gone.
And even more, she gives.
She reaches out to the hurting.
It's a one-way street, painful always,
as she walks it barefoot,
and still, she thanks the gravel.

Each day, a new war.
Each smile, a small defiance.

And yet, she wonders, will she ever be held
without conditions?
Will another's arms ever open for her
just because she exists?
Will her name ever taste like love
on someone else's tongue?

She prays, sometimes.
I pray too.

Still,
she rises.
Not always proud, but always upright.
On days like this,
as she gathers herbs and flowers, the beautiful gifts from Gaia.
Sun-warmed and fragrant,
pressing them gently to the places that hurt.

Her heart.

Her Soul Number 7 reminds her, there is wisdom in pain.
Her Life Path 2 whispers, you were made for peace.
Her Expression 9 cries out, 'you are here to transform all that hurt into healing'.

She listens.

Slowly,
gently,
she turns her face to the light.
It won't last,
the battle always returns.
But today, for now, she is held by the sun,
and for a moment,
she is more than okay.

That woman,
all brave, but broken,
a beautiful soul beyond belief…

That woman is me.

SHAZ E NEWMAN

IT'S A ONE-WAY STREET,
PAINFUL ALWAYS,
AS SHE WALKS IT BAREFOOT,
AND STILL...
SHE THANKS THE GRAVEL.

THE THREAD BETWEEN US: MY SIBLINGS AND ME.

I am the middle one.
A daughter: a sister stitched between two sons.
The scapegoat.
The silence.
The shadow child, without a place to shine.

My older brother, a fierce spirit in a failing frame.
He was my twin in sorrow, my mirror in pain.
Together, we navigated the bruised corners of our childhood,
dragging light through the cracks whenever we could.
He left too soon at 27.
I was 25.
And the ache he left behind, is still my second skin.

I built a house for him, brick by dream,
window by hope, but he never did come home.

Then there was my younger brother,
bright, distant, a constellation away.
I left when he was only eight.
And time, so unforgiving, widened the quiet.

Years later, the numbers found me.
Carved me open.
Offered meaning.

Three siblings.
Three versions of the same truth: all a Life Path 11/2.
The Seeker.
The Sensitive.
The soul that feels a little too much.

We walked the same path, but in different shoes.

My older brother:
11/2 with a 6 Expression,
the loyal one, heart-led, a giver, even when the world took more
than he had.

Me:
29/11 with a 9 Expression,
the ache-keeper, the one who tried to carry it all,
even the pieces no one wanted.

My younger brother:
38/11, Expression 7,
the quiet one, thinking from a distance,
a fortress, behind those careful, dark brown eyes.

We each held a thread from the same cloth.
The same number, but a different pattern.

I built him a house, my older brother.
Poured it from hope, from need, from the ache of
wanting to give him more
than what we had as children.

Four walls, open skies, a room with light enough
to melt away those years.

I thought,
If I could build it, he would come, and we could start
again.
Find breath,
find freedom, find a life, the one I thought we should
have.

But he never made it.
And the house stayed hollow.
Just like me.

Still, he visits.
Not in my dreams, but in the numbers.

He was always the carer,
even in pain.

Even in silence.
Even in leaving.

And I …
Well, I see it now.
Maybe the house wasn't for him.
Maybe it was a place to lay it all down.
To find a way back to myself.

I used to think I didn't belong.
That I was the wrong note in our family song.

Perhaps I was, perhaps I am, but lately I see things differently,

And I know...
I was the thread.
The witness.
The one who remembered all that we couldn't say.

We were broken, and yet we weren't,

We were just different expressions of the same life lessons.

Three became two.
Two became one.

And somehow,
that was always the path.

The numbers held the map, we just didn't know how to read it yet.

Our lives, shaped by the same quiet rhythm.
Our roles, written in the margins long before we arrived.

Now I walk for all of us.
Still listening for the signs.
Still holding what was never said.

We were never truly separate.
Just three echoes of the same soul story.
Still connected.
Still walking home.

SHAZ E NEWMAN

The blood of a thousand roses.

Unless you heal,
you will bleed,
on those, that didn't cut you.

I was always the rose,
that grew from concrete.
Something beautiful,
amongst the tarmac.

Yet my suffering,
didn't come from my struggle.
It came from trying to run.
Shackled by
the weight of the world,
There was no fun.

The longer I avoided the pain,
I was left to wither and shrink,
I did not see,
I was to blame.

I saw their beauty,
but not the shards.
The longer I held on,
I broke my heart.

Dying to save others.

I chose to heal for all those,
who suffered,
when they didn't cut me.
Yet those I love,
still bleed on me.

I see only beauty,
but my hands are scarred.
From the thorns,
they keep as guards.

I can only heal,
so I no longer bleed,
on those I love.
Where I've planted seeds.

Yet I still rescue,
the withered roses.
That didn't heal,
I drown in their blood.
For they refuse to feel.

KIKI

The Collective Proposal.

Let's make a promise collectively.
When we glance in the mirror to be gentle and kind,
To learn and to grow, and to nurture our mind.
To love our body, every freckle and curve,
And to give ourselves the praise we lovingly deserve.

Let's make a promise, collectively.
To support other women and straighten their crown,
To raise each other up, without tearing anyone down.
If you fail to find kind words, because you're having a bad day,
Remember, spite leaves a nasty taste, so just walk away.

Let's make a promise, collectively.
No one walks alone, no matter the fight,
We hold hands tight, through the blur of the night.
Hearts may clash, but safety comes first,
Sisterhood shields us, from facing the worst.

Let's make a promise, collectively.
To stand up for what we believe, even if we stand alone,

Because peace will follow, when our truth is known.
If the place you're in, no longer feels right,
Create your own space, your people will find your bright light.

Let's make a promise, collectively.
To be kind and understanding, let compassion be your guide,
But set your boundaries clearly and never let them slide.
Know your values, make your rules, stay true without regret,
Honour what you stand for, and don't you dare forget.

Let's make a promise, collectively.
To understand that our love can't be bought,
There's nothing you owe, no favour to be sought.
We ask for respect, as all hearts deserve,
And kindness returned with the care that we serve.

Let's make a promise, collectively.
To share our stories with the world, to encourage and inspire,
For every woman silenced, your strength she does desire.
Your voice is needed; strong, sincere, and true,

In speaking your truth, you light the way too.

Let's make a promise, collectively.
To be strong, to be brave, to be thoughtful and smart,
To be all the things that you value, whilst following your heart.
To be grateful, creative, and open to play,
Our time here is limited, so make the most of each day.

Let's make a promise, collectively.
We are daughters, friends, sisters and mothers,
But remember self-care is the foundation of giving to others.
Step into the sunlight, breathe in the fresh air,
And pass this promise on to all women, and continue to share.

SARAH JENKINS

WE ARE WARRIORS,
SCARRED BUT BRIGHT,
WE BURN AWARENESS,
INTO LIGHT.

The Cry Beneath the Smile

Fourteen years, I carried pain,
Misread, dismissed, it had no name.
'Just IBS', they always said,
While a hidden illness quietly spread.

Endometriosis, chronic, cruel,
Invisible scars, no textbook rule.
One in ten, yet still denied,
Behind my smile, how much I cried.

It's not 'just a period', not 'just fatigue',
It's waking to pain, each breath a siege.
Friends drift away, I cancel again,
Too sore to talk, too drained to explain.

I've tried it all, pills and more,
Birth control, to close a door.

They said surgery would clear the path,
But pain returned, came roaring back.
Laparoscopies, they cut, they seared,
Yet this disease is never cleared.

No cure in sight, just a line of trial,
Hormones, side effects, a long hard mile.

Menopause before my time,
Or a choice too heavy, too steep to climb.

But still I rise, soft, yet steel,
I speak the truth, they tried to seal.
For those like me, who've felt alone,
Your pain is valid, your strength well-known.

We are warriors, scarred but bright,
We burn awareness into light.
Misdiagnosed, misunderstood,
Together now, we make them listen good

So here's my voice, no longer hushed,
A soul too strong to ever be crushed.
Unseen, yes, but never undone, we fight together,
This pain has lasted far too long.
Awareness grows with every word,
And now, we will be heard.

JACKIE HALL

The Dragon Mandala

You arrive at the circle of your becoming.
Flowers and leaves bloom at your feet.
Tree stalks rise beside you,
growing before your eyes.

Magic hums in your chest.
Your heart expands.
Twinkling lights dance all around.

The earth breathes you in.
Roots stretch from your feet into the path.
The colour of life rises,
unlocking the green door of your heart.

Beside you, the river glimmers,
starlight rippling on water,
though the sun is still high.
Dragon wings beat in the distance,
keeping time with your heart.

Ahead, trees weave a tunnel,
threads of light drifting like seeds.
Dragonflies hum,
butterflies greet you,
each carrying a dream.

Toadstools cluster at the roots,
scarlet caps, white speckles.
They rise as you walk,
inviting you to the world between worlds.

The air shifts.
Warmth brushes your skin,
scented with ember and earth.
Golden eyes gleam through the branches.

The dragon emerges,
scales of green, copper, gold, and moss.
Wings fold into the archway.
A claw extends,
offering a key.
light woven with shadow,
strength bound with gentleness,
threaded with fairy tea.

It drops into your palm.
It fits the lock you carry in your soul.

Ahead, the portal shimmers,
green and gold,
twinkling with light.
Beyond, a ribbon of gold loops into infinity,
the dragon's flight,

your own awakening.

You step through.
Magic and morning dew fill your breath.
Your heartbeat sends ripples through the mandala,
waves of colour and firelight.

The dragon's gaze lingers,
not as guardian,
but as mirror.
The mandala turns once more.
You stand at its centre:
rooted, radiant, awake.

KRIS DAVIES

The Painting

A picture that stirs our mind and our senses remember
A vision that awakens us out of our slumber
A temporary moment special to behold
A story hidden and now ready to be told

Sitting in stillness taking in the view
I'm here in the moment, maybe one of a few
Listen to the quiet, feel the dryness in the air
Giving ourselves permission to enjoy some self-care.

Feel the tranquillity of stillness
Treasure the wonder of the scene
Watch the sun dip below the horizon, as if in a dream
The hues of pinks, orange and gold above us, the sky ablaze
Reflecting in the surroundings, casting a magical haze

A picture painted from the heart of another
It's impact far reaching beyond that was thought
Let the smile of the memory lighten up your face
Taking you back to that cherished place

Lisa Harwood

THE PAUSE

(Between Mother and Crone - My Queendom)

I am standing here
in the pause…
        the place between worlds.
        Where the crown is not handed to you
                but forged from the ash
                of every fire
                you thought would burn you to
nothing.

This is not the girl's becoming.
That season has long passed.
        This is the deep breath
        between the inhale of mothering all things
                and the exhale of sovereign rule
                over the land of my own spirit.

I have birthed children
dreams
revolutions.
        I have mended bones
        stitched heart-skin with shaking hands
                carried lovers, families, strangers
                through storms with no name.

I have known the scent
of my own blood in the dirt
    and learned to call it sacred.

Now, the Mother in me loosens her grip.
She hands me the map of my scars
    the ledger of what I gave away, and says…
    'This is the last time you will labour
        for a kingdom built to keep you hungry.'

We were never meant to rule in palaces
drafted by the hands of patriarchy.
    Our thrones rise from the earth…
    where roots run deep
        and the crown feeds the heart
        as much as the head.

I strip down to the raw truth:
I am not what I do for others.
    I am the architect of a throne
    no one else can sit upon…
        carved from boundaries
        that open inward
            to the wild, green centre of me.

I have traversed hemispheres
to return to the land of my ancestors.

Soil that remembers my name
Where my body is no longer a battlefield
but the temple of my choosing.

Here I listen for the old songs
of the women who walked before me...
their footsteps warm on the earth
their laughter stitched into the wind.

They tell me:
You are the queen now.
Not the kind who waits to be chosen
but the kind who knows
this crown is her birthright.

So I gather my tools:
Truth. Wisdom. Faith...
to see the unseen
hear the unheard
feel the mystery
touch the darkness
and still choose light.
Tears, to water the ground.
Fire, that knows when to burn
and when to warm.

I plant my staff in this soil and claim it:

This Queendom is mine.

Still… this is only the pause…
the in-between
        where the seed remembers it is not the dirt
        and the chrysalis learns
                the dark is part of the dance.

Soon, I will step out crowned and certain
hips swaying with the rhythm
        of a woman who belongs to herself.

For now, I stand in stillness
feeling the shift of worlds within me.

        The pause is not an ending.
        It is the throne room door.

                And I am already inside.

KAREN SMITH

This Thing Called Love

If an alien came down from up above, and asked us, *'What's this thing called love?'*

We would not talk of hearts and flowers, nor fluttering butterflies.

We'd share the joy of a slow Sunday morning; cosy blankets pulled tight, warm cuddles and tousled hair.

Where everyday love lives in small acts of teamwork; you wash the dishes, hands warm from soft soapy bubbles, whilst I create your favourite dish, wearing pink fluffy slippers.
We chat about our day and our frustrations, and then pause mid conversation and share a smile. A tell-tale sign that everything, will work out fine.

Love is the small acts of kindness, no one else sees. A drink in case I get thirsty, a blanket to keep me warm, your favourite snack at the end of the day, when the world's been unkind and words drift away.

When the weight of the world grows heavy, the

sound of your calm voice, your gentle touch, lends me the strength to carry on.
Together we cherish the joys of parenting; the hidden laughs, the silent fears, the memories etched across the years. A token of the love we share.

So, when asked, *'What's this thing called love?'* We won't speak of grand gestures or dramatic displays. We'll smile and simply say; love is sharing a life with your best friend, the one who sees you, knows your flaws and stays.

SARAH JENKINS

TO CHALLENGE EVERY
DUSTY SYSTEM,
THAT WAS NEVER BUILT
WITH US IN MIND.
TO BUILD MENTAL WEALTH,
NOT JUST
MENTAL HEALTH.

Mirror, Mirror on the Wall

Oh, how I wish I was a mirror on the wall.

So when you walk by
and turn your gaze
so you can't see.

I could tell you
what beauty is before me
the outer and the inner.

To reflect back
what the world can see
but you ignore.

How your eyes shine
when you're excited.

How your energy
transmutes sadness
into happiness.

How the way you talk
etches into our soul
and embeds hope.

Oh, how I wish I was a mirror on the wall.

To wipe away your, I can't do's
I'm not enough
I'm not worthy.

To show you all the ways
the world already sees
that you can
that you are enough
that you are so worthy.

To wipe away any of your pains
and help you feel
how your presence touches this world
just by being you.

Oh, how I wish I was a mirror on the wall.

To show you
how amazingly epic you really are.

And that this world
would not be the same without you.

KELLIE VVIND

As I Rise

I used to shrink when I felt full,
Censor my ache, my time, my rising,
I believed softness meant sacrifice to feel meaningful,
I thought that cycles meant a time for hiding.

But the moon has never once,
Apologised for being whole,
For being too dark or too much,
Or too bright to hold.

I stopped grieving the ones,
Who wanted my flame,
But flinched from the heated sun,
And when they burned, I was to blame.

Lovers who drank from my magick,
But could not stay for the storm,
Who kissed my crown but called me tragic,
My darlings, no longer will I mourn.

Like sovereign, I cast them away from my altar,
Not in anger, but in ritual.
The reclamation of my body will never falter,
Every single inch I now call, beautiful.

I loved the maiden.
I embrace the mother.
And I intend to walk beside the wise woman.

I call myself divine, finally free.
I name my body a temple.
I sing to the mirror until she believes in me.
Let those who sought to see me fall, now tremble.

The goddess has my back as I rise,
I am ready for the world to truly see,
I will not bow, nor compromise,
For the moon's fierce fire lives in me.

CLARY A WILDE

Together We Rise

In the heart of Wales - where valleys sing.
A sisterhood blooms. A powerful spring.
Women's Academy Wales - a beacon, bright.
Reigniting our purpose. Dreams in our sight.

When self doubt whispers, we find voices that soar.
As we gather as one, to discover our core.
With resets and retreats, we help map the way.
Empowered together, come what may.

Beth's the career guide, she helps us rewrite our story,
Navigating life's challenges to find our glory.
With heart and strength, she helps women grow,
To own their worth and let it show.

Andrea's the oracle on confidence anew,
Teaching us to find a voice that's true.
She urges us to face our fears,
To speak with strength, to strangers or peers.

Emma's our ultimate wellness muse,
Showing us how to heal, to thrive, to choose.
She helps us to reset and repair,
Healing mind and body with powerful care.

Together they lead with passion and grace,
Creating a kind and nurturing space.
With each connection, our spirits lift,
In shared experiences, we discover a gift.

So here's to the women, who dare to dream,
To build, to lead, to form a team.
No longer confined by roles of old,
Let's step fiercely into stories untold.

WOMEN'S ACADEMY WALES

Dragons Child

Under Samhain's silvered shadows,
Reborn in the embers of the Dragon's breath,
Between the veils, of this world and the other,
Takoda emerged.
Ak'ab'al duality between darkness and light, the transition between night and day.
New beginnings, opportunities and hidden knowledge.
Slipping from dreams to dawn, transition to awareness,
Transformation, life, death and rebirth.

In the West, Autumn, the Earth, cradling the quiet endings,
In the North, Winter, the Air, winds whispering my stillness.
In the East, Spring, the Fire, carrying songs of beginnings,
In the South, Summer, the Water, emotions, teaching me joy.
I walked in all directions, many times, over many years, rainbows arching over me,
Mother Earth below, Grandfather Sky above and ancestors all around me.

I learned to dance with Dragons, who have sat and
flown beside me,
Playing barefoot in the meadows, paddling in the
streams.
Collecting frogspawn, watching tadpoles grow and
frogs jump away,
Foraging wild herbs, fungi, plants and berries.
Talking with the spirits, flora and fauna, fae folk and
ancestors,
I earned their respect and learned their speech.

I have been the Maiden, the quiet muddy girl with
scuffed knees,
I have been the young women, in the shadows.
I have laughed so hard, my ribs and cheeks hurt,
I have cried, the grief so much, but was never lost.
I have danced barefoot in the rain, sat in nature,
wondering how to begin again,
I heard the breath, the drum, the heartbeat of the
universe.
I have been the Mother, the friend, the giver, the
wanderer across ancient lands and cosmos,
Through it all, the longing, the leaving, the laughter,
the letting go.
I have remained a dreamer, intuitive, creative and
kind,
I hear my own soul's song.

I am the Crone, still here, making a difference, still learning every day.

GAYNOR GENT

So when they ask,
'What's wrong with you?'
I smile, and answer
with something true:
What's wrong with me?
'Nothing, you see...
Perhaps you're just, wrong for me.'.

We Are Not Done

One moment, sunshine danced on my skin,
no cares, no clouds, just light within.
Then without warning, the winds turned cold, and
everything I knew began to fold.

Life twisted, cracked, and came undone,
the ground beneath me on the run.
A jelly world, I slip and slide, trying to stand while
waves collide.

Plans once golden, dreams once near,
now blur behind a veil of fear.
But even as the sky turns grey,
hope whispers softly, *'Find your way.'*

The unknown looms, yet still I try,
with tear-stained cheeks, I look to the sky.
For life was never meant to stay,
it bends, it breaks, then lights a way.

So I hang on tight, heart open wide,
while dancing on this shifting tide.
And though it hurts, I still believe,
in joy ahead, in love received.

I'm learning now to trust the flow,
to plant new seeds and watch them grow.
Even in grief, there's space for grace,
a softer rhythm, a slower pace.

And maybe this edge is where I rise,
with fire in soul and open eyes.
The story's not done, the page will turn,
and in the ashes, embers burn.

But I am not walking this road alone,
there's a hand in mine, a steady home.
Two hearts,
one fight,
come what may,
we hold each other through the grey.

Because through it all, we've not lost ‘we’,
we hold the light so tenderly.
Calm, while rivers rage inside,
walking hand in hand through every tide.

We may not know what lies ahead,
but we choose love, not fear, instead.
In the face of storms we can't outrun,
we stand, we sway...

We Are Not Done.

Zoe Newth

We Sing To The Sea

We step forward.
Bare feet on cold stones.
Holding our breath between courage and surrender.

The sea waits.
Not gently,
with a knowing presence, she does not promise comfort.

Drawn in, we enter.
A gasp, a sharp cry,
laughter breaks like sunlight though the waves.

We sing to the sea.
Not with melodies,
but with shouts, squeals and shuddering exhalations.

Joy meeting fear.
She answers a hush.
A pull of something deeper, salt born and raw.

Clare Thalassa

What Nana's Say...

For mine - the rainbow in my grey sky

What Nana's say,
stays with you.
Long after the biscuits are gone,
the cushions reshaped,
and her familiar scent has faded.

She doesn't shout her wisdom,
she stirs it lovingly into the tea,
neatly folds it into freshly washed towels,
quietly whispers it, while brushing your fringe, from
your eyes.

My Nana had this way,
like the world could be on fire,
and she'd still make it feel safe.
She'd sit me down,
look straight into my little overthinking heart,
and say:
'Shall we sprinkle some 'wait and see' powder on it?'
And just like that,
my storm would soften.

It wasn't magic, not really.

It was presence.
It was love, steady and fierce,
wrapped in soft cardigans and the smell of home.

They've lived full lives, our Nan's.
Been daughters, lovers, mothers,
carried guilt and grief, they never speak of.
And now, with silver hair and softer hands,
they get a second chance,
to love in a way they maybe didn't know how to, the first time round.

No rushing.
No yelling.
No *'because I said so.'*
Just eyes that see straight through the mess,
and hearts big enough to hold all your worry,
without needing to fix it.

They remember what it's like to be small,
to be scared,
to feel too much.
And somehow,
without needing to say a word,
they make you feel like,
you were never too much at all.
So when I worry, I still hear her,

even now.
'Let's sprinkle some 'wait and see' powder on it'
And I smile.
Because what Nana's say,
stays, always!

Hayley Perkins

WHAT'S WRONG WITH YOU?

Since I can remember, one question would sting:
'What's wrong with you?' - like a bell they'd ring.
I was a little girl, seeing more than I should,
Reading truths in their faces, the bad and the good.

Asking the questions they didn't want heard:
'Why lie to the people you claim to have stirred?
Why hurt the hearts you're meant to defend?
Why call me lovely when all you intend,
Is to get close to my mother's trust?'

'What's wrong with you?' they'd say in disgust.
What's wrong with me? I'd whisper inside,
Why did my presence feel like a crime to hide?

Growing up, I was curious, wild with flame,
but that wasn't part of my parent's game.
'You must mind your sisters, be the example we need.'
So I turned my bright energy inward, unseen.

'What's wrong with you?' they'd always repeat.
What's wrong with me? - my steady heartbeat.

Teenage years came with a glittering cure,

a quiet for the chaos I couldn't endure.
Life of the party, but hollow within,
smiling outside while I wore thin.
Feeling the pulse of everyone near,
yet always alone, when the noise would clear.

'What's wrong with you?' they'd laugh or sigh.
What's wrong with me? I'd silently cry!

Adulthood arrived - the noise grew loud,
I tried to fit in, to blend with the crowd.
The more I played 'normal', the more I would ache,
the more I longed for an endless escape.

'What's wrong with you?' they'd smirk and say.
What's wrong with me? - I'd push away.

The fear, the noise, the hurt turned black,
the truth I was missing, bent my back.
Alone in crowds, alone in the night,
escaping in ways I knew weren't right.

I walked through places that weren't my own,
paths of destruction I should have outgrown.
Hating myself for being 'too much' and 'too small',
never enough - yet somehow, too all.

WHAT IS WRONG WITH ME?
And then - one word: AuDHD.
Could this really, explain me?
I read and I wept, I learned and I grieved,
for the life I had lost, the self I'd believed.
For the dreams that had died, the signs I'd missed,
for the moments unlived, for the love dismissed.

Now, I have a map, I have a key,
a truth that finally lets me, be me.
Too much for some, not enough for a few,
but perfectly enough for the ones who see true.

I live with love, with purpose, with grace,
I stand unshaken in my own space.

So when they ask, 'What's wrong with you?'
I smile, and answer with something true:
What's wrong with me? Nothing, you see…
Perhaps you're just, wrong for me.

VERONICA SOMMARIVA

Reflections

When I looked at your reflection,
You weren't even there,
When I looked at your reflection,
All I could do was stare.
The changes I needed,
Reflecting on the past,
The changes so scary,
So big and so vast.
The visions of the future,
Were small and uninviting
But with some work,
They are now so exciting.
You were told what you weren't,
You were told that you couldn't,
Not to see your own worth,
You thought it meant that you shouldn't.
The reflections are new now,
They are still scary,
But deep down you know,

You deserved a life, less ordinary.

Alison Worrall

WHILE I SLEEP

While I sleep
I do not weep
While I sleep
I do not think
While I sleep
I dream of good times gone by

While I sleep
I see an Angel in the sky
While I sleep
My heart won't ache
While I sleep
I make no mistakes

While I sleep
I don't have to think about tomorrow
While I sleep
My whole being will not be filled, with sorrow

While I sleep
I see your beautiful face
While I sleep
I feel comfort from your silent embrace

While I sleep
I don't have to make promises, that I can't keep

While I sleep
I know you're by my side
While I sleep
There is no turning tide inside
While I sleep
It's always yesterday

While I Sleep

DEBBIE ANNE TURNBULL MBE

So find your own rhythm,
a path you can trace,
And make time for well-being,
in your own sacred space.

Who would you be?

Who would you be if your parents, family, friends ideas, had not been drip fed to you slowly, through the passage of time, from the womb, until you grew into adulthood?
All the well meaning rules of society coming from so many angles.

Who would you be if the world wasn't playing out it's own story?
If you didn't have to be entwined in others life?
People in your world, impacting your thoughts, feelings and your actions.
Involved with drama, leading to creation of your own.

Who would you be if you refused to fit into the mould, the mould that has been shaped for you?

Who would you be if you allowed yourself to be free, not worrying about others judgement?

Who would you be? Who were you really meant to be?

The person who will never really be…

Wendy Stoneham

Unstoppable Impact

Why do I do this work?
Because I've stood in the ashes of my own becoming,
cracked open but still standing.
Because I know how trauma wears red lipstick,
how burnout hides in the boardroom,
how people-pleasing feels like safety,
when your nervous system is screaming, *survive.*

I do this because I was her,
the woman who led in silence,
achieved in overdrive,
and smiled through soul-deep exhaustion.

Because quick fixes don't free us.
Plasters don't patch, pain soaked in the
subconscious.
So I fused neuroscience with soul,
strategy with surrender,
hypnotherapy with heat,
and called it, *transformation.*

I'm not here to 'cope'.
I'm here to crack the code.
To challenge every dusty system,
that was never built with us in mind.

To build mental wealth, not just mental health.
To remind women that healing is a power move,
and legacy is louder than trauma.

I've walked through prison gates and palace halls.
I've sat with CEOs and survivors.
And I've learned this:
Visibility is powerful, but voice?
Voice is where revolutions begin.

So if you feel me, know this:
I'm not here for likes.
I'm here for liberation.
I'm not here to be impressive.
I'm here to be impactful.
And I am no longer asking for permission.

This is not a moment.
It's a movement.

Let's rise.

NICOLA NOÉL

WHY TRY?

Why try, what's the point of the fight,
When shadows fall and block your light?
When all you achieve in success draws envy, not cheer,
And kindness is met with a whispering sneer?

I dreamed and I dared,
my career was my fire,
Fuelled by ambition, by hope and desire.
The thrill of the spas,
where my talents would shine,
A-list names on my schedule, this craft was mine.
Each treatment I gave was my personal art,
With pride in my hands, and care from my heart.

But then came a moment, that threatened it all,
My hands bore a burden which challenged my all.

At this crossroads, I carved a path brand new,
A business with purpose that steadily grew.
To support my income, I taught on the side,
Not just to speak, but to mentor with pride.

Opportunities came, I gave it my heart,
And built something steady, right from the start.

Through challenge and change,
I stayed true to my route,
Watching futures unfold, nurturing youth.

Whispers and envy began to behave,
Like shadows that grew with each effort I gave.
I stood firm, with kindness and grace,
But cold shoulders met me,
They turned from my face.

I gathered my strength, and tried something new,
Fresh faces and methods, where my confidence grew.

Then out of the blue came a knock on my door,
A new chance to lead, to build something more.
Someone had seen my values and creed,
I was what they wanted,
I was in need.

Betrayal returned, and cut even more,
From someone I trusted, this hurt to the core.
Each day was a battle, soaked in despair,
Why try, when it feels like, there's nobody there?

But deep down I knew, through the struggle and strain,
That I had the power to rise once again.

I turned to what mattered,
the skill that still burned,
A business with heart, where respect was earned.

No titles, no noise, just passion and care,
Rebuilding my future with purpose laid bare.

Now I surround myself with those who are true,
No users, no takers, just genuine few,
who give as I give, and see as I do.

So why try?
Because trying brings hope, when the road feels unclear,
It gives us direction, it silences fear.
This next chapter's mine,
the page has been turned.
With each step I take, I'll use all that I've learned.

ANGELA L POWELL

Womb of Light

A Healing Journey into Motherhood

I healed my womb with sacred breath,
With quiet tears, with loving depth.
I held my pain in open hands,
And planted hope in shifting sands.

Two souls arrived, a whispered pair,
One stayed earthbound, one filled the air.
My angel baby, born to sky,
You dance in dreams where spirits fly.

My Earth-side love, you breathe and grow,
A heartbeat, I have come to know.
And in your eyes, so wide and bright,
I see your twin, in morning light.

I healed my womb, with moon and flame,
Through ancient grief, and holy name.
From loss and longing, raw and deep,
I rose, I wept, I learned to keep.

The love of both, who called me 'home',
One here beside me, one has flown.
Yet both are mine, in soul and skin,

My angel child, my Earth-born twin.

This path was carved, by ache and flame,
But I emerged, and claimed my name.
I am the mother, soft and strong,
With lullaby and warrior song.

I healed my womb. I made it whole.
I birthed new life. I grew my soul.
This is my truth, my sacred flood,
This is my light. This is my blood.

SOPHIE POWELL

Wonders of Well-being

Our body, mind, and soul, what a team!
A living, breathing, beautiful dream.
This three-part wisdom, so clear & true,
A new way of being, now opens for you.

The body's a home, a temple we keep,
In water, good food, and restful sleep.
A gut-brain hums, a wise, deep part,
Producing calm for a happy heart.

The magical mind can get all caught,
With busy thoughts and lessons it's taught.
So give it a moment, just to be still,
And let imagination and dreams fulfil.

The soul is our spirit, a peaceful flame,
It just wants kindness, to whisper its name.
With gratitude's light, and a hand to lend,
It finds a purpose, that has no end.

It's all connected, a powerful flow,
What we do for one, helps the others to grow.
So find your own rhythm, a path you can trace,
And make time for well-being, in your own sacred space.

Lisa May Barker

Please Forgive Me

Please forgive me, if ever I have done you wrong. Please know it was never my intent. I was lost in battles you could not see, facing wounds not yet spent. Shadows of a past unhealed, whispers of pain held tight. I walked through storms within my soul, searching blindly for the light.
So please forgive my moments weak, my silence, my misplaced fear. This journey of the spirit calls for lessons year by year.
And for all who've wounded me, whether knowing or unaware, I release the weight, I let it go, with love beyond compare. For sometimes, life is all too much, a tide that pulls us deep. But I choose to rise, to free my heart, from sorrow I won't keep.
I forgive you, I forgive myself, no chains will bind us now. Let's let it all dissolve like mist, no past shall break our vow. A vow to heal, to love, to grow, to rise above the pain. To walk this path with open hearts, and never break again.

Lisa Williams

ALL THIS TIME

You thought it was you, too weird and too much,
Too quick to love, too soon to trust.
You blamed yourself when he turned away,
And words cut deep or fists would sway.

Their minds were closed, they looked, then turned,
Too safe, too numb, too unconcerned.
You second guessed, your every tone,
And wore the fault like it was known.

Some saw it all, but stayed away,
Their silence louder every day.
But what they missed, the stars have kept,
The Universe watched every step.

You smiled through storms, to seem okay,
You made excuses, shrank each day.
You softened truth, ignored the ache,
And dimmed your light for their mistake.

The body stored, what time dismissed,
A buried wound, a clenched up fist.
It echoed on, through years unspoken,
A soul entangled, split and broken.
But then anger came, began to flame,

It named the grief, it called the shame.
It rose and burnt inside your chest,
Not to destroy, but to release the mess.

So breathe it out, the weight, the sting,
The voice that questions, everything.
You lived it. Felt it. Broke the chain,
You've nothing to prove through this pain.

You're not what happened, not the rage,
You are the fire, they couldn't cage.
And now at last, you shine, refined and bold,
Each broken piece rewoven, with strength and gold.

VICKIE THOMPSON

I HOPE YOU FIND YOUR PEOPLE,
AND I HOPE THEY LET YOU IN.

WE'VE GOT YOU

The path that isn't straightforward
When people block your way.
The route that seems so challenging
You want to give up for another day.

Then suddenly it becomes clear
As you see the sisterhood by your side.
The ones that walk beside you.
Your faithful loyal guides.

For when you find your circle
The tribe that lifts you up.
The energy that surrounds you
Overfills your cup.

The route ahead is now exciting
Each step driving and defining you.
Yes there will still be challenges
Yet you know that you'll get through.

You'll hear us whispering *'We're here too'*
Supporting any path you choose.
We understand your feelings
For we've once walked in your shoes.

You don't walk this earth as a lone wolf
Your pack is always nearby.
Ready to be your wings when needed.
You are the empress soaring high.

JULIE M GRABHAM

Dear Daughter

In your eyes, I see a reflection of my life's pain.
I see the world you are going to see.

I try to calm myself,
I erupt with grief,
Knowing what is to come for you.

Heart ache so bad, you'll want the world to end.
Bullying so horrible, you'll want to retract in to the shadows.
Grief so piercing, you'll want to pierce yourself.
Self doubt so crippling, you'll question who you are.
Self loathing so intense, you'll want to change your smile.

I don't know how to protect you.
I don't know how I can change it.

I will fill you with confidence, ammunition, words, strength and self love.
But I know it's going to come.

I want you to be…

Be strong,

be a fighter,
be kind,
be happy,

…be better than me.

I want you to always understand that I am here.
I'll never stop being here.
I am here forever.
For you.

Mama Buca x

SAMANTHA BUCA

I Hope You Find Your People

I hope you find your people, the ones who speak to your soul, who hear the quiet in your voice and help you feel whole. The ones who light the dark days, who stay when others roam, who see the cracks and love you more, who makes this world fee,l like home.

I hope you find your circle, where laughter runs in streams, where every flaw is welcome, and silence still hold dreams. May they see you with clear eyes, no masks, no need to hide, and may you feel their embrace, that you are known inside.

So when the road is lonely, and hope feels faint and thin, I hope you find your people, and I hope they let you in.

Lisa Williams

ACKNOWLEDGEMENTS

To my beloved *Nanny Peggy,* thank you for your love and wisdom on this earth, and now as my guardian angel. You have guided me every step of the way, leading me to create this book to honour our voices.

To Stephanie Starla of Starla Publishing House, your unwavering support and sacred space-holding carried me through every version of myself in this process. I could not have done this without you. You are a true creative goddess.

To the 111 women who bared their souls within these pages - thank you for your love, courage, strength, and wisdom. This book breathes because of you.

And to my beautiful daughter, Bethany-Grace, may you always carry the love in your heart to follow your dreams, and may you always know, you are more than enough.

About Lisa Williams

Lisa is a Spiritual Creative Mentor, Kundalini Reiki Master, dance teacher, author, and podcaster.

She is the heart behind the Spiritual Sisters Collective, a loving community that uplifts and empowers women around the world.

Through her workshops, classes, and retreats.

Lisa gently guides women back to themselves, helping them uncover their strength, creativity, and joy.

A Closing Note

Every day we find ourselves moving through
different rhythms.
Sometimes fast, sometimes slow.
Sometimes bright, sometimes heavy.

Wherever you are, and whatever season you are
moving through right now,
please remember this truth:

You are loved. You are worthy. You are enough.

Let these words be an anchor to your soul.
Carry them with you, and return whenever you need
reminding.

If any of the themes within RHYTHM: Poetry For
Your Soul have touched tender places in your heart,
please don't walk through them alone.
Reach out to someone you trust, a loved one, a friend.

And if you need more support, there are safe, caring spaces and services available for you:

Mind UK – for mental health support:
www.mind.org.uk | 0300 123 3393

Samaritans – available 24/7 to listen:
www.samaritans.org | Call 116 123

Child Bereavement UK –
support for children and families:
www.childbereavementuk.org | 0800 02 888 40

May you continue to find your rhythm,
again and again,
always guided by love.

The Light With Me, Celebrates The Light With You.

Lisa.

Printed in Dunstable, United Kingdom

71812929R10180